ANCIENT EGYPT

ART AND ARCHAEOLOGY
OF THE LAND OF THE PHARAOHS

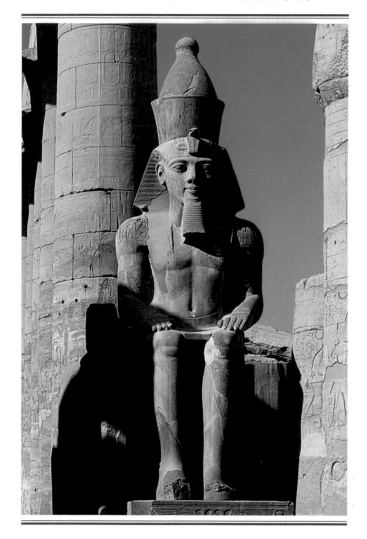

GIORGIO AGNESE

MAURIZIO RE

BARNES
& NOBLE
BOOKS

NEW YORK

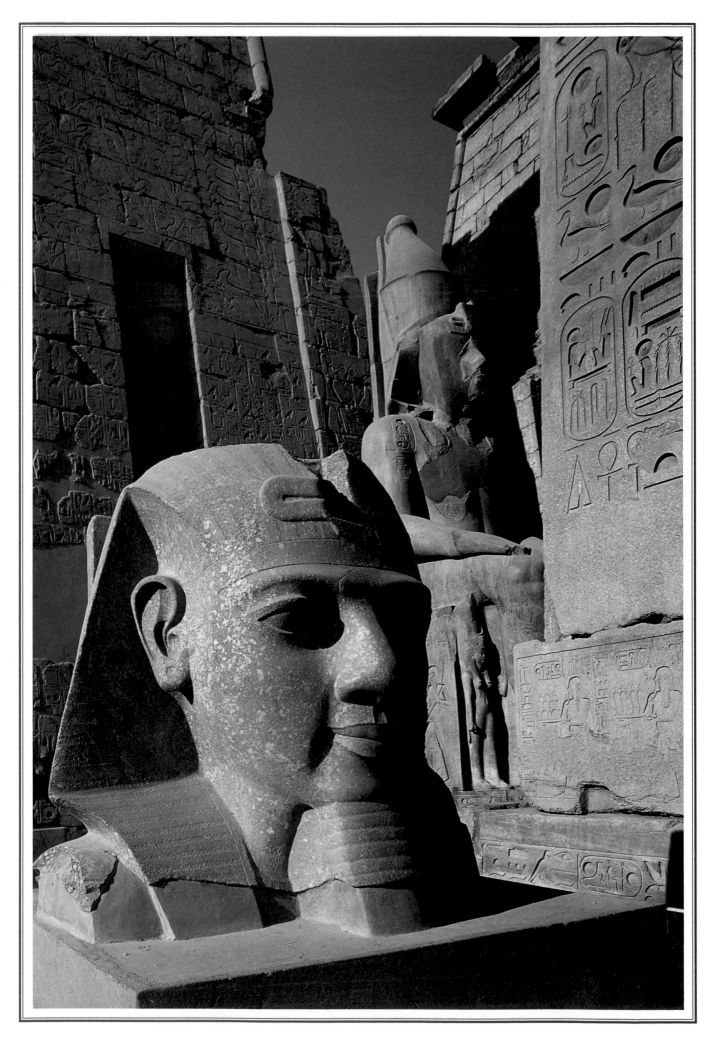

ANCIENT EGYPT

TEXT
Giorgio Agnese
Maurizio Re

GRAPHIC DESIGN
Paola Piacco

TRANSLATION
Neil-Frazer Davenport

Contents

1
One of the colossi of Rameses II
in the temple at Luxor.

4
A colossus head of Rameses II
in the temple at Luxor.

2-3
The Sphinx and the Pyramid
of Khafre at Giza.

5
The solid gold death mask
of Tutankhamun.

QATTARA
DEPRESSION

Libyan Desert

OASIS OF BAHARIYA

EGYPT

6 top left
A fleet of feluccas sailing on the Nile.

6 bottom left
An aerial view of the Nile near Luxor.

OASIS OF
DAKHLA

Libya

6 top right
The temple of al-Dakke, reconstructed on the shores of Lake Nasser.

6 bottom right
The oasis of El Feyran, overlooked by Gebel Tahuna, in the Sinai peninsula.

*Sahara
Desert*

Israel

ALEXANDRIA   PORT SAID

Delta of the Nile   ISMAILIA

GIZA   CAIRO   SUEZ

SAQQARA

FAIYUM

Sinai

Jordan

AQABA

ABU ZANIMAH

Saudi Arabia

ST. CATHERINE

Gulf of Suez

SHARM EL-SHEIKH

7

A view of the magnificent cliffs near Sharm el-Sheik.

Nile

Arabian Desert

ASIS OF KHARGA

ABYDOS

DENDERA

WEST THEBES

KARNAK/
LUXOR

ESNA

EDFU

KOM
OMBO

ASWAN

Lake Nasser

ABU SIMBEL

Asia Minor

Israel

Egypt

Saudi Arabia

Red Sea

Africa

Atlantic
Ocean

Madagascar

Indian
Ocean

8-9

This view from space shows the luxuriant Nile Valley. The meander in the foreground corresponds to the Luxor area.

8 bottom

Another two views from space in which the Red Sea (left) and the Sinai peninsula (right) are clearly visible.

Preface

For obvious practical reasons, condensing all the information of general interest concerning Egypt into a small volume—without neglecting important facts—is by no means easy. Prepararing a concise yet exhaustive text dealing with Egyptian archaeology is all the more arduous given the number and vastness of the sites and monuments found in the country and the fact that the ancient civilization lasted for over 4,000 years. The selection of sites included in this book comprises all the major tourist attractions, while the historical-archaeological aspects of the monuments mentioned are treated at some length.

The territory inhabited by the ancient Egyptians is that which we see today, consisting of the Nile valley between the Mediterranean to the north and the second cataract south of Abu Simbel. The river traces a fertile strip over 600 miles long. This strip is delimited on either side by desert areas which are in turn flanked by arid hills and mountain ranges separating it from the Red Sea to the east and the Sahara to the west. In the north, close to modern-day Cairo, and in

proximity to ancient Heliopolis and Memphis, after having flowed for 4,039 miles the great river branches out into the delta that in ancient times was green with vegetation but swampy and impassable. Before the building of the Aswan dam, in fact, the river rose annually, flooding the countryside and leaving the prevailing winds and the sun with the task of drying out land which would emerge covered with a new layer of silt rich in humus and mineral salts.

The lifestyle of the inhabitants of the Nile valley was essentially agricultural. Still today, sailing upstream from Cairo the landscape you encounter is little different from the one that existed thousands of years ago. *Kemet* was the name the ancient Egyptians gave to their land: black land, fertile land, the gift of the gods and the deified river Nile.

This ancient civilization which survived for millennia was rediscovered and studied in depth only relatively recently. We already know much, but archaeology still has plenty to reveal and Egyptology still has to provide answers to questions regarding several obscure periods in Egypt's history and numerous unresolved mysteries.

9 top
This photograph clearly shows the Faiyum, the Nile Valley, and the Sinai peninsula.

9 center
The Nile Delta, seen from space.

10-11
Aerial view of the temple complex at Luxor.

9

Historical Introduction

12 top

A soapstone disc from the tomb of Hemaka at Saqqara. 1st Dynasty.

12 center left

Top, a fragment of the Libyan Tribute Palette, from Abydos, Protodynastic Period; bottom, jar with painted decoration, Predynastic Period.

In 1998, the Egyptologist Guenter Dreyer of the German Institute of Cairo discovered two bone tablets at Abydos in the tomb of an ancient sovereign known to the Egyptologists as the "Scorpion King." The two tablets bear a form of archaic writing and are datable to around 3400 B.C., while the Narmer Palette, previously considered to be one of the earliest documents of Ancient Egypt, has instead been dated to 3000 B.C.

Given that the culture of ancient Egypt was not actually extinguished until around A.D. 400, when the knowledge of hieroglyphic writing was lost and the pagan cults were banned from the country, the Egyptian civilization lasted around 4,000 years, an episode unique in human history.

The area of ancient Egypt had been inhabited from the prehistoric period. In the post-glacial era only two geographical zones were particularly favorable to the development of a civilization. One of these was the upper valley of the Nile, extending to the south of Africa, and the second comprised present-day Turkey and Mesopotamia and extended as far as the Indus River.

The first Neolithic agricultural communities settled in the upper Nile valley and the oases around 7-8,000 years ago. These cultures, defined as "predynastic," enjoyed a rapid organizational, social, and technological (metallurgy) development before the start of the dynastic epoch inaugurated with the first historical pharaoh Menes (Aha) who, tradition has it, unified a country previously divided into northern and southern sectors.

The reality was rather more complex. Archaeological finds testify to the existence of a nameless king (known as the "Scorpion King" after the figure appearing on a ceremonial mace) who reigned at the end of the predynastic period between 3150 and 3050 B.C. Many Egyptologists place the Scorpion King in the so-called Dynasty 0 along with Narmer, perhaps the father of Menes. The Museum of Cairo contains the votive Narmer Palette, the most famous find related to this king, discovered at Hierakonpolis (the ancient city of Nekhet) by the American archaeologist Quibell in 1897.

According to Herodotus (whose writings are supported by archaeological research), the pharaoh Menes is attributed with the construction of Memphis, the capital of the unified kingdom at the apex of the Nile delta. The city was protected by a

dam designed to deviate the course of the river and avoid the annual flooding of the houses. It is interesting that the kings of this dynasty chose Abydos as their burial ground, the necropolis of the first capital of the country, Thinis. The aristocracy instead had their tombs built at Saqqara. Aha's tomb at Abydos is located in the northwestern necropolis, together with that of his presumed wife Benerib.

The people were frequently exploited and kept in poverty. The discontent this generated inevitably led to increasingly serious internal struggles and a complete undermining of the sovereign's authority. In what was now an ungovernable country, a new feudal-style system was developing. This period included the Seventh-Tenth Dynasties (2152-2065 B.C.) and is defined as the First Intermediate Period. It was not until the Twelfth Dynasty and the reign of the Pharaoh Amenemhat I (1994-1964 B.C.) that central power was reinforced at the expense of the sacerdotal class. The capital was moved to It-towi (not far from Lisht) and work began on the expansion of the irrigation system at Faiyum. There followed the period of Senusret I, Amenemhat II, and Senusret II and III who

14
Diorite statue of Khafra, from Giza. 4th Dynasty.

15 top left
Ivory statuette of Khufu, from Abydos. 4th Dynasty.

15 bottom right
Triad of Menkaura in grey-green schist, from Giza. 4th Dynasty.

The Third Dynasty (2649-2575 B.C.) opened with the Pharaoh Sanakht (Nebka) who is less well known than his presumed brother Djoser, the builder of the step pyramid in the central sector at Saqqara (circa 2600 B.C.). In reality this monument was designed and built by the vizier Imhotep, something of the Leonardo da Vinci of his era and elevated to almost divine status by subsequent generations.

We have far more information about the Fourth Dynasty thanks to archaeological finds. The period saw the reigns of the pyramid-building Pharaohs Sneferu, Khufu, Khafre, and Menkaura, and was one of the most remarkable epochs in history, with Egypt distinguished by an elevated level of social, cultural, and artistic organization. The pharaoh was at the top of the hierarchical pyramid, with the sacerdotal class wielding great political power a step lower. For administrative purposes, the territory was divided into regions known as *nomes*, and entrusted to members of the aristocracy, the *nomarchs*. With the passing of time, the sacerdotal class and the sub-divided wielders of temporal power acquired increasing autonomy with respect to the central power of the sovereign and did not always exercise their power over the population properly.

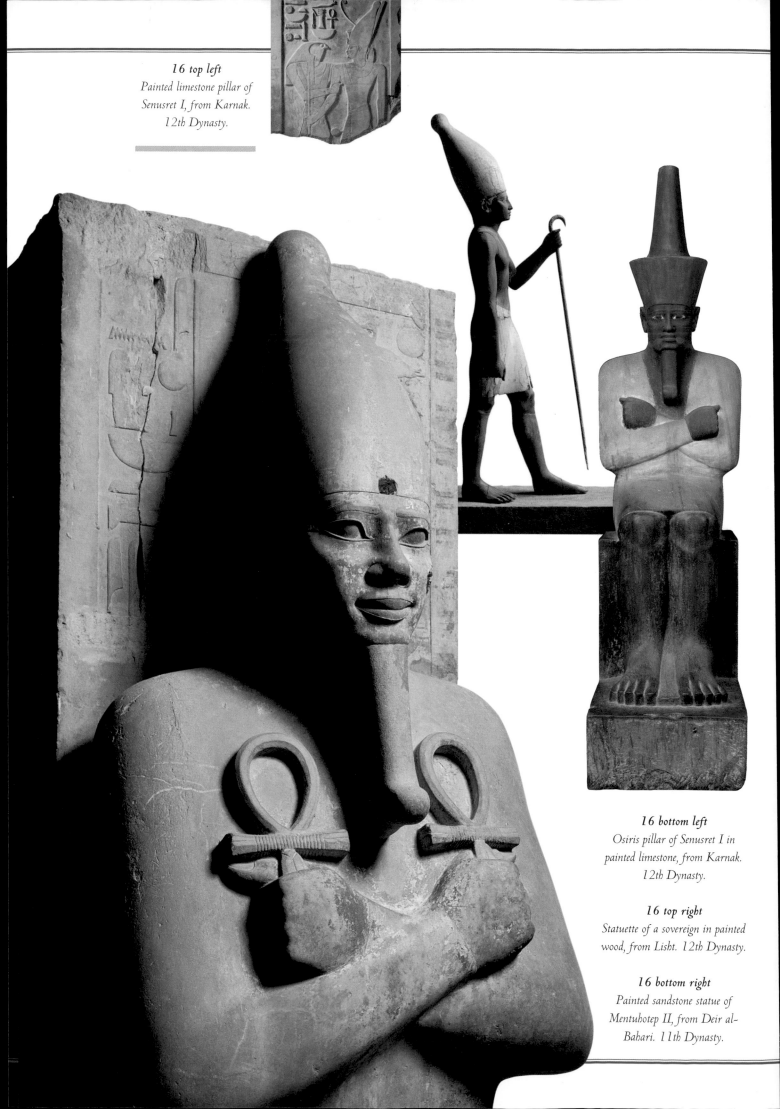

16 top left
*Painted limestone pillar of
Senusret I, from Karnak.
12th Dynasty.*

16 bottom left
*Osiris pillar of Senusret I in
painted limestone, from Karnak.
12th Dynasty.*

16 top right
*Statuette of a sovereign in painted
wood, from Lisht. 12th Dynasty.*

16 bottom right
*Painted sandstone statue of
Mentuhotep II, from Deir al-
Bahari. 11th Dynasty.*

extended the Egyptian borders towards the Middle East and conquered Nubia with its rich deposits of gold.

The Middle Kingdom (2065-1650 B.C.) was a particularly fertile period for sculpture, the working of gold, and civil and military architecture. In fact, the Egyptians themselves referred to this as a "golden age." It is no coincidence that in the celebrated novel by Mika Waltari, Sinhue the Egyptian is set in this period of splendor.

Literature, above all, enjoyed considerable development and the texts of the period were copied by the successive generations. The works produced during the Middle Kingdom frequently contained intellectual concepts handed down from the Old Kingdom, a fact which has allowed modern scholars an insight into the most remote aspects of Ancient Egyptian knowledge.

The applied sciences also found fertile terrain in the Middle Kingdom and specialized medical, mathematical, and veterinary treatises were written. The construction of pyramids was revived, albeit on a smaller scale (Lahun), while the largest temple of all

time, mentioned by Herodotus in Book II of his History as the "labyrinth," was also built.

The Twelfth Dynasty drew to a close with the Pharaoh Amenemhat IV and Queen Sebeknefru (1781 B.C.) and from this point the historical reconstruction becomes fragmentary and confused. There was a period of transition (the Second Intermediate Period) that, perhaps as a result of the weakness of the pharaohs of the Thirteenth/Fourteenth Dynasties, saw the gradual infiltration of the Nile delta by nomads of Semitic origin, perhaps arriving from the Asiatic steppes. These people were called the Hyksos, a name deriving from the Grecian form of Heka-Kasutt (heads of foreign countries).

The capital of Egypt was moved to Avaris (Hat-Uart) in the Nile delta. The Hyksos domination of Egypt lasted around 250 years and spanned the Fifteenth, Sixteenth and Seventeenth Dynasties which saw numerous successive pharaohs of whom only a few names and rare works are known.

18 top

Head in painted limestone from an Osiris colossus of Queen Hatshepsut, from Deir al-Bahari. 18th Dynasty.

18 bottom

Interior of the Hathoric chapel built by Thutmosis III at Deir al-Bahari, today conserved in the Egyptian Museum of Cairo. 18th Dynasty.

The Second Intermediate Period concluded around 1550 B.C. with the accession of Ahmose I, the progenitor of the Eighteenth Dynasty during which Egypt was finally freed from foreign domination.

This period, the so-called "New Kingdom," saw great monarchs such as Queen Hatshepsut, Thutmosis III, one of the greatest Egyptian sovereigns and warriors, and Amenhotep IV, better known as Akhenaten, the creator of the so-called "Amarna heresy" who introduced the cult of the solar disc Aten. Then came the boy-king Tutankhamun, famous for his tomb full of treasures.

The period of rebirth and prosperity continued into the Nineteenth Dynasty (1291-1185 B.C.) with the reigns of great Pharaohs Sety I, Rameses II, and Merneptah who left testimony to their power in the

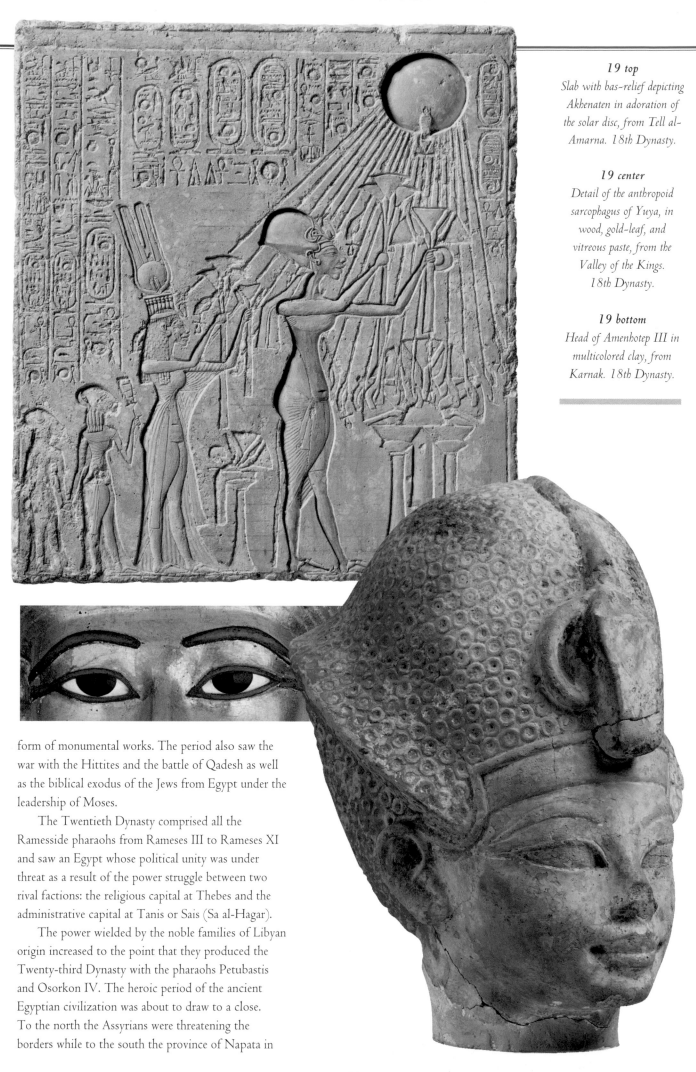

form of monumental works. The period also saw the
war with the Hittites and the battle of Qadesh as well
as the biblical exodus of the Jews from Egypt under the
leadership of Moses.

The Twentieth Dynasty comprised all the
Ramesside pharaohs from Rameses III to Rameses XI
and saw an Egypt whose political unity was under
threat as a result of the power struggle between two
rival factions: the religious capital at Thebes and the
administrative capital at Tanis or Sais (Sa al-Hagar).

The power wielded by the noble families of Libyan
origin increased to the point that they produced the
Twenty-third Dynasty with the pharaohs Petubastis
and Osorkon IV. The heroic period of the ancient
Egyptian civilization was about to draw to a close.
To the north the Assyrians were threatening the
borders while to the south the province of Napata in

20
Detail of alabaster canopic vases from the tomb of Tutankhamun in the Valley of the Kings. 18th Dynasty.

21 top
Detail of the alabaster colossal statue of Sety I, from Karnak. 19th Dynasty.

21 bottom left
Top, gold pendant in the form of Isis, from Tanis; bottom, gold basin with handles belonging to Psusennes I, from Tanis. 19th Dynasty.

21 bottom right
Relief with Rameses II holding his enemies, from Memphis. 19th Dynasty.

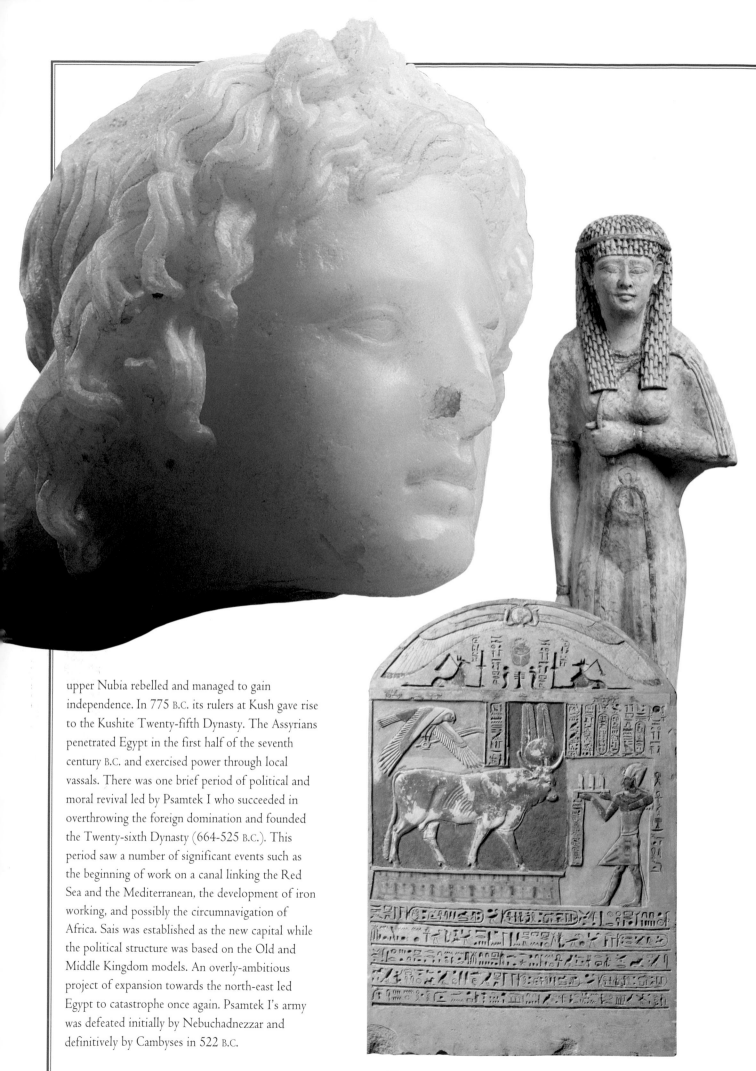

upper Nubia rebelled and managed to gain
independence. In 775 B.C. its rulers at Kush gave rise
to the Kushite Twenty-fifth Dynasty. The Assyrians
penetrated Egypt in the first half of the seventh
century B.C. and exercised power through local
vassals. There was one brief period of political and
moral revival led by Psamtek I who succeeded in
overthrowing the foreign domination and founded
the Twenty-sixth Dynasty (664-525 B.C.). This
period saw a number of significant events such as
the beginning of work on a canal linking the Red
Sea and the Mediterranean, the development of iron
working, and possibly the circumnavigation of
Africa. Sais was established as the new capital while
the political structure was based on the Old and
Middle Kingdom models. An overly-ambitious
project of expansion towards the north-east led
Egypt to catastrophe once again. Psamtek I's army
was defeated initially by Nebuchadnezzar and
definitively by Cambyses in 522 B.C.

22 left
*Small alabaster head of
Alexander the Great, from
al-Yauta. Ptolemaic Period.*

22 top right
*Painted and gilded statuette
of a Ptolemaic queen, from
Karnak. Ptolemaic Period.*

The Persian dynasties reigned until 332 B.C.,
when Alexander the Great defeated the Persian
king Darius III. The Greek conquest marked the
onset of the decline of the ancient culture and
dragged the country into a new dimension
dominated by a radically different school of
thought.

On the premature death of Alexander in 323 B.C.,
the government of Egypt was entrusted to Ptolemy,
the son of Lagos, who in 304 B.C. became pharaoh
with the name Ptolemy I Soter. Ptolemaic Egypt
enjoyed another period of prosperity as the policies
introduced led to social renewal and economic
development, marked by notable architectural and
artistic works such as the temples of Denera, Edfu,
Kom Ombo, Esna, and Philae. Many of these
monuments have survived to the present day.

Alexandria became the center of Greek culture in
the Mediterranean, while Hellenism spread throughout
the known world from the Egyptian port. The ancient
Egyptian culture, whose roots dated back millennia,
nonetheless managed to keep its religious traditions
alive. These traditions were combined with those of
the Greeks, giving rise to new forms, partly because the
ancient religion was always tolerated and respected by
the conquerors. The pantheon of divinities was
expanded and the artistic canons survived, albeit in a
more modern, "revised" form. Alexandria itself was,
however, already infused with the new Hellenist culture.

There were fifteen Ptolemaic pharaohs, including
two women, Berenice IV and Cleopatra VII. The last
of the line was Ptolemy XV, the son of Caesar and
Cleopatra, perhaps better known as Caesarion.
Following the suicide of Cleopatra and the execution
of Caesarion by Octavian Augustus, Egypt became a
province of the Roman empire. The Romans also
greatly admired Egyptian culture and such was the
emperors respect for the ancient traditions that they
had themselves crowned and took the divine title of
pharaoh.

The passion of Egyptian exoticism reached such a
height that the worship of Isis and other esoteric cults
was taken up in Rome and became particularly popular
among the upper classes.

22 bottom right
*Stela of Ptolemy V in
painted and gilded
limestone, from Armant.
Ptolemaic Period.*

23
*Presumed portrait of
Cleopatra in white marble.
Ptolemaic Period.*

25 top
*Detail of the sarcophagus of
Yuya, from the Valley of the
Kings. 18th Dynasty.*

25 bottom
*Pictorial detail from the
tomb of Nefertari in the
Valley of the Queens.
19th Dynasty.*

Chronology

PREDYANSTIC PERIOD
(4000 - 3000 B.C.)

Naqada I (4000 - 3500)
Naqada II (3500 - 3100)
Dynasty 0 (circa 3000)
Narmer

PROTODYNASTIC PERIOD
(2920 - 2575 B.C.)

1st Dynasty (2920 - 2770)
Aha (Menes ?)
Djer
Djet
Den
Adjib
Semerkhet
Qa'a
2nd Dynasty (2770 - 2649)
Hetepsekhemuy
Raneb
Nynetjer
Peribsen
Khasekhem
(Khasekhemwy)

OLD KINGDOM
(2649 - 2152 B.C.)

3rd Dynasty (2649 - 2575)
Sanakht 2649 - 2630
Djoser (Netjerkhet)
2630 - 2611
Sekhemkhet 2611 - 2603
Khaba 2603 - 2600
Huni 2600 - 2575
4th Dynasty (2575 - 2465)
Snefru 2575 - 2551
Khufu 2551 - 2528
Djedefra 2528 - 2520
Khafre 2520 - 2494
Menkaura 2494 - 2472
Shepseskaf 2472 - 2465
5th Dynasty (2465 - 2323)
Userkaf 2465 - 2458
Sahura 2458 - 2446
Neferirkara Kakai
2446 - 2426
Shepseskara 2426 - 2419
Neferefra 2419 - 2416
Nyuserra 2416 - 2392
Menkauhor 2392 - 2388
Djedkara Isesi
2388 - 2356
Unas 2356 - 2323
6th Dynasty (2323 - 2152)
Teti 2323 - 2291

Pepy I 2289 - 2255
Merenra 2255 - 2246
Pepy II 2246 - 2152

FIRST INTERMEDIATE PERIOD
(2152 - 2065 B.C.)

7th Dynasty
A shadow dynasty. Manetho mentions "seventy kings of Memphis who ruled for seventy days" to indicate the period of confusion through which Egypt passed.

8th Dynasty (2152 - 2135)
About twenty ephemeral Memphite sovereigns are known. Qakara Aba, whose pyramid still stands at Saqqara, is the only king historically acknowledged.
9th and 10th Dynasties
(2135 - 2040)
Dynasties in which the government of much of Egypt passed into the hands of the city of Hierankleopolis, before the Theban Dynasty took power again.
11th Dynasty - first part
(2135 - 2065)
Mentuhotep I
Antef I
Antef II 2123 - 2073
Antef III 2073 - 2065

MIDDLE KINGDOM
(2065 - 1781 B.C.)

11th Dynasty - second part
(2065 - 1994)
Mentuhotep II
Nebhepetra 2065 - 2014
Mentuhotep III
2014 - 2001
Mentuhotep IV
2001 - 1994
12th Dynasty (1994 - 1781)
Amenemhat I 1994 - 1964
Senusret I 1964 - 1929
Amenemhat II
1929 - 1898
Senusret II 1898 - 1881
Senusret III 1881 - 1842
Amenemhat III
1842 - 1794
Amenemhat IV
1793 - 1785
Queen Nefrusobek
1785 - 1781

SECOND INTERMEDIATE PERIOD
(1781 - 1550 B.C.)

13th Dynasty (1781 - 1650)
Around seventy ephemeral sovereigns who reigned very shortly.
14th Dynasty (1710 - 1650)
An unknown number of ephemeral sovereigns all coeval to 13th and 14th Dynasties.
15th Dynasty (1650 - 1550)
Main Hyksos kings:
Salitis
Sheshi
Yaqobher
Khayan
Apopi
Khamudi
16th Dynasty (1650 - 1550)
Minor Hyksos governors ruling at the same time as the 15th Dynasty.
17th Dynasty
(1650 - 1550)
Fifteen Theban sovereigns, the most important of whom are:
Antef V
Sobekemsaef I
Sobekemsaef II
Antef VI
Antef VII
Seqenenra Tao I
Seqenenra Tao II
Kames

NEW KINGDOM
(1550 - 1075 B.C.)
18th Dynasty
(1550 - 1291)
Ahmes 1550 - 1525
Amenhotep I 1525 - 1504
Thutmosis I 1504 - 1492
Thutmosis II 1492 - 1479
Hatshepsut 1479 - 1458
Thutmosis III 1479 - 1425
Amenhotep II
1424 - 1397
Thutmosis IV
1397 - 1387
Amenhotep III
1387 - 1350
Amenhotep IV/
Akhenaten 1350 - 1333
Smenkhkara
1335 - 1333
Tutankhamun
1333 - 1323

Ay 1323 - 1319
Horemheb 1319 - 1291
19th Dynasty (1291 - 1185)
Rameses I 1291 - 1289
Sety I 1289 - 1279
Rameses II 1279 - 1212
Merneptah 1212 - 1202
Amenemes 1202 - 1199
Sety II 1199 - 1193
Siptah 1193 - 1187
Tausret 1193 - 1185
20th Dynasty (1187 - 1075)
Sethnakht 1187 - 1184
Rameses III 1184 - 1153
Rameses IV 1153 - 1147
Rameses V 1147 - 1143
Rameses VI 1143 - 1135
Rameses VII 1135 - 1127
Rameses VIII 1127 - 1126
Rameses IX 1126 - 1108
Rameses X 1108 - 1104
Rameses XI 1104 - 1075

THIRD INTERMEDIATE PERIOD
(1075 - 664 B.C.)

21th Dynasty (1075 - 945)
Smendes I 1075 - 1049
Neferkara 1049 - 1043
Psusennes I 1045 - 994
Amenemope 994 - 985
Osorkon the Elder
985 - 979
Siamon 979 - 960
Psusennes II 960 - 945
22th Dynasty (945 - 718)
Sheshonq I 945 - 924
Osorkon I 924 - 899
Sheshonq II 890 circa
Takelot I 889 - 883
Osorkon II 883 - 850
Takelot II 853 - 827
Sheshonq III 827 - 775
Pimay 775 - 767
Sheshonq V 767 - 729
Osorkon IV 729 - 718
23th Dynasty (820 - 718)
Petubasty 820 - 795
Sheshonq IV 795 - 788
Osorkon III 788 - 760
Takelot III 765 - 756
Rudamun 752 - 718
24th Dynasty (730 - 712)
Tefnakht 730 - 718
Boccori 718 - 712
25th Dynasty (775 - 653)
Alara 775 - 765
Kashta 765 - 745

Piankhy 745 -713
Shabaqo 713 - 698
Shabataqo 698 - 690
Taharqo 690 - 664
Tanutamani 664 - 653

LATE PERIOD
(664 - 332 B.C.)

26th Dynasty (664 - 525)
Psamtek I 664 - 610
Nekau 610 - 595
Psamtek II 595 - 589
Apries 589 - 570
Amasis 570 - 526
Psamtek III 526 - 525

27th Dynasty (525 - 404)
Cambyses 525 - 522
Darius I 521 - 486
Xerxes I 486 - 465
Artaxerxes I 465 - 424
Xerxes II 424
Darius II 423 - 405
Artaxerxes II 405 - 404

28th Dynasty (404 - 399)
Amirteus 404 - 399

29th Dynasty (399 - 380)
Nepherites I 399 - 393
Hakor 393 - 380

30th Dynasty (380 - 342)
Nectanebo I 380 - 362
Teos 362 - 360
Nectanebo II 360 - 342

31th Dynasty (342 - 332)
Artaxerxes III 342 - 338
Arse 338 - 336
Darius III 336 - 332

HELLENISTIC PERIOD
(332 - 30 B.C.)

The Macedonians (332 - 305)
Alexander the Great
332 - 323
Philip Arrhidaeus
323 - 317
Alexander IV 317 - 305

Ptolemaic Dynasty (305 - 30)
Ptolemy I Soter
305 - 282
Ptolemy II Philadelphus
285 - 246
Ptolemy III Euergetes
246 - 222
Ptolemy IV Philopator
222 - 205
Ptolemy V Epiphanes
205 - 180

P. VI Philometor 180 - 164,
163 - 145
Ptolemy VII Neos
Philopator 145
P. VIII Euergetes
170 - 163, 145 - 116
P. IX Soter 116-110,
109-107, 88-80
P. X Alexander
110 - 109, 107 - 88
Ptolemy XI Alexander 80
P. XII Neos Dionysos
80 - 58, 55 - 51
Berenice IV 58 - 55
Cleopatra VII Philopator
51 - 30
Ptolemy XV Cesarion
36 - 30

ROMAN PERIOD
(30 B.C. - 313 A.D.)
*Only the names of the emperors
mentioned in the hieroglyphic and demotic
texts are cited.*

Augustus 30 B.C. - 14 A.D.
Tiberius 14 - 37
Caligula 37 - 41
Claudius 41 - 54
Nero 54 - 68
Galba 68 - 69
Otho 69
Vespasian 69 - 79
Titus 79 - 81
Domitian 81 - 96
Nerva 96 - 98
Trajan 98 - 117
Hadrian 117 - 138
Antoninus Pius 138 - 161
Marcus Aurelius 161 - 180
Lucius Verus 161 - 169

Commodus 180 - 192
Septimus Severus 193 - 211
Caracalla 198 - 217
Geta 211 - 212
Macrinus 217 - 218
Diadumenianus 218
Alexandrer Severus 222 - 235
Gordian III 238 - 244
Philip 244 - 249
Decius 249 - 251
Gallus and Volusianus
251 - 252
Valerian 253 - 260
Gallienus 253 - 268
Macrianus and Quietus
260 - 261
Aurelian 270 - 275
Probus 276 - 282
Diocletian 284 - 305
Maximian 285 - 305
Galerius 293 - 311
Maximin Daia 305 - 313

The Gods of Ancient Egypt

From religious and philosophical points of view, the Egyptians conceived the world as the valley in which they lived, or rather a land that developed vertically from south to north rising from the waters, just as out of the waters of Nun, the primordial ocean, were born the earth and the heavens. The other dominant element of this world that originated from water was the sun, the power of which was capable of baking the land and withering crops as well as bringing life, light, and warmth.

Just as the waters of the Nile flowed northwards from the south, the earliest inhabitants of Egypt saw the sun rise and set on a trajectory from east to west that intersected that of the river. Each evening, the sun disappeared in the west as if had been swallowed by the sky, and during the night it was regenerated and appeared again the next day on the eastern horizon. From the earliest of times, the Egyptians used these simple natural observations to develop a vision of a world based on the terrestrial north-south and celestial east-west

26 top
Rameses II, depicted twice, prostrates himself before the solar disc. Drawing taken from Ippolito Rosellini's Religious Monuments.

26 bottom
The crocodile god, Sobek, in a drawing taken from Ippolito Rosellini's Historical Monuments.

26-27
Rameses II before Amun-Ra, Mut, and the divine form of himself, from the Temple of Abu Simbel. Drawing taken from Ippolito Rosellini's Historical Monuments.

axes which formed the foundation of their religious beliefs.

Curiously, as vital as the Nile was to their very existence, and despite the part it played in their vision of the world, the Egyptians never deified it, associating with divinities not the river itself but rather its effects. Thus, they identified Hapi, a god associated with the concept of abundance, with the phenomenon of the Nile flood, and similarly, the energy of the waters that revitalized and fertilized the land was associated with the resurrection myth of Osiris. Hence the correlation between the cult of the dead, the concept of divine resurrection, and the fertilization of the land that was probably developed as early as the Predynastic Period.

N.º LXXXVI.

27 top
The god Ra-Harakhti, in a drawing taken from Ippolito Rosellini's Historical Monuments.

27 bottom
Sety I introduced by Horus before Osiris and Imentet. Drawing taken from Ippolito Rosellini's Historical Monuments.

28-29
Offerings and libations to the god. Tomb of Ramesses III, Thebes. Drawing taken from Historical Monuments *by Ippolito Rosellini.*

The Egyptians believed that the Nile flowed from a cavern, fed by the subterranean ocean of Nun, itself composed of the primordial waters from which the universe was created and on which the world floated. They thought that the great river flowed uninterruptedly towards the very waters that fed it and returned to the surface in an eternal and immutable cycle of regeneration. They also believed that the sun god Atum-Ra, creator of all things, rose out of the primordial ocean Nun. In turn, the sun created two deities—Tefnut, the damp air and Shu, the dry air—who then created the god Geb (the earth) and the goddess Nut (the sky). Out of the union of these last two came the gods Osiris, Isis, Seth, and Nephthys. This conception of the world is a recurrent motif in

many images in which Nut is depicted as a naked woman, elongated and supported by the god Shu to prevent her from falling onto her consort Geb, depicted as a sleeping, naked man. Each evening, Nut swallowed the solar disc and gave birth to it once again in the morning. Not infrequently, her body was depicted covered with stars.

The Egyptians' religious beliefs were very complex and their pantheon was populated by a multitude of different deities. In general, it may be said that ancient Egyptian culture in its entirety was permeated by religion: society itself was structured according to a rigid hierarchy, from the gods to the pharaoh through to the people subdivided into classes. The gods personified the forces of nature, supervising every event and every activity. They were responsible for the destiny of the country and its every inhabitant. The cults of the various gods were the responsibility of the pharaoh and the priests who provided for the terrestrial needs of each deity and the care of their material images according to extremely complex rituals. The people instead venerated their gods in small tabernacles and shrines constructed in the villages and the countryside. Moreover, each region, district, and settlement had its own gods and its own myths which were accepted with absolute tolerance by the official clergy.

The minor deities (actually the most important in terms of popular religion) manifested themselves in multiple forms and took diverse names from place to place. Egyptologists have identified several thousand. The Egyptian people had a practical conception of religion and associated every natural phenomenon with a particular deity who might take the form of animals, plants or natural events. Frequently, animals such as cats, crocodiles, and bulls were mummified and placed in special necropolises after their deaths. Among the

30 right
*Also part of
Tutankhamun's funerary
furnishings, this golden
necklace counterpoise,
with semiprecious stones
and vitreous enamel
features some figures
representing eternity.*

gods worshipped throughout Egypt were Osiris, the Lord of the Underworld portrayed in the form of a mummy with a bluish flesh tone, his wife Isis, a witch and powerful goddess of life and regeneration, the jackal-headed Anubis, the god of the necropolises and patron of mummification, and Bes, depicted as a dwarf with monstrous features, the protector of pregnant women and god of the family.

Among the secondary deities most frequently encountered in Egyptian iconography are Maat, the goddess of justice, represented with a feather on her head, Khum, the god who modeled man on his potter's wheel, represented with a ram's head, Seth, the god of negativity and destruction, represented with the head of an unidentifiable animal, Hathor, the goddess of love, the arts, and music, represented with the ears of a cow, Bastet, the beneficent goddess and protector of births, represented with the head of a cat, Thot, the god of writing and notary to the gods, represented with the head of an ibis, and Sobek, a god who protected the waters from enemies, represented with the head of a crocodile. Lastly, the deities venerated above all at Thebes, were the triad composed of Amun-Ra, king of the gods, and the solar deity, Mut, his wife, and Khonsu, their son and the god of the moon.

31 foreground
*Detail of a pectoral
depicting the goddess Nut,
in gold, cornelian, and
vitreous enamel. This jewel
is from the tomb of
Tutankhamun, too.*

31 background
*This relief depicting the
goddess Isis with her wings
outspread decorates
Tutankhamun's inner
sarcophagus in solid gold.*

The Cult of the Dead

The evidence discovered by archaeologists demonstrates that ever since the Neolithic period, the inhabitants of Egypt had a profound belief in the existence of a spirit world in which the deceased would have needs similar to those they had known during their terrestrial existence.

It was actually in Egypt, in the first half of the third millennium B.C., at the time of the Third Dynasty, that the first true monumental tombs in history were built.

If in the Protodynastic Period the royal tomb was already strictly connected to the affirmation of terrestrial power, by the time of the Third Dynasty, the tomb had also become a symbol of the pharaoh's divinity and of his power and celestial capacity to overcome death from which the whole country could benefit. To express these new concepts, Imhotep, Djoser's great chancellor and architect, designed the first stepped pyramid at Saqqara which symbolized a staircase towards the sky allowing the pharaoh's celestial ascension. This is an idea expressed on a number of occasions in the *Pyramid Texts*, collections of formulas and prayers that are found inscribed in the pyramids from the Fifth Dynasty onwards and which subsequently evolved into the *Sarcophagus Texts* and the *Book of the Dead*.

32-33
Funeral scenes from Theban tombs. Drawings taken from Ippolito Rosellini's Civic Monuments.

Djoser's successors also adopted the concept of the pyramid-tomb which, during the reign of Snefru, the first pharaoh of the Fourth Dynasty, acquired its definitive form as an expression of the ever greater importance attached to the solar cult in association with that of royalty. Because the religious concept had evolved, the celestial staircase was no longer necessary: the steep sides of the pyramid, a manifestation in stone of the sun's rays, similarly allowed the pharaoh's spirit to reach the sky.

During the New Kingdom (1550-1075 B.C.), the Egyptian sovereigns, having abandoned the use of the pyramid form for royal tombs, had immense burial chambers dug into the rock and decorated with magical-religious texts. Their contents would allow the deceased king to overcome the innumerable dangers that he would encounter on his journey through the underworld before joining the sun god Ra, of whom he was believed to be a son. Because the journey through the underworld was so perilous, the dead were accompanied by numerous amulets. Moreover, it was thought that a

particularly delicate phase existed between the moment of death and the true passage to the underworld, during which divine judgement that not even the pharaoh could avoid, took place. The deceased, brought before the gods Osiris and Anubis, saw his own heart weighed by the god Thot on scales counterbalanced by a feather, the manifestation of Maat, the goddess of order and justice. If the two plates of the scales were balanced, then the deceased had been upright and honest during his terrestrial life and deserved to be welcomed by Osiris in the next world; otherwise, the spirit was devoured by a terrible monster and annihilated forever.

All of the New Kingdom's magnificent underground tombs contained fabulous funerary furnishings, as the tomb of Tutankhamun demonstrated. The funerary caches were considered to be crucial to making life in the underworld more pleasant and thus included everyday objects, furniture, games, and foods of all kinds. Moreover, the tombs also contained special

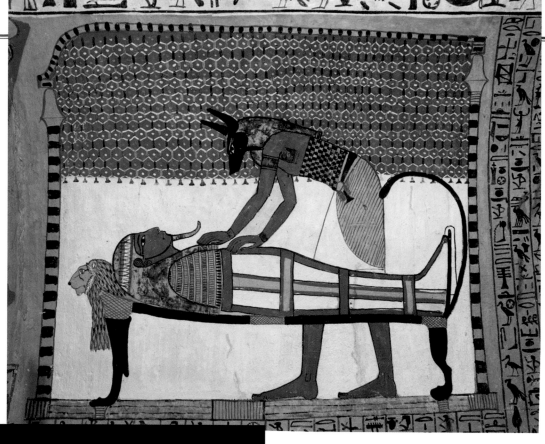

34 top
The god Anubis, intent on embalming a corpse. Wall painting from one of the Tombs of the Nobles.

34 center
Four painted limestone vases carrying the name of Yuya and discovered in the Valley of the Kings. 18th Dynasty.

34 bottom
The "Tribune of Osiris" from the tomb of Rameses VI in the Valley of the Kings. Drawing taken from Ippolito Rosellini's Religious Monuments.

statuettes (*ushabti* figures) that, once brought to life in the underworld, would have obeyed the orders of the dead and completed the most onerous tasks in his place.

A large, richly appointed tomb was not the exclusive privilege of members of the royal family, but one also of high ranking dignitaries and even simple artists and craftsmen. They also had highly ornate tombs, although the decorative motifs were different to those of the royal tombs and were inspired by scenes of daily life rather than of the underworld.

The characteristic that differentiated the civilization of ancient Egypt from all the others which developed in the Mediterranean basin and the Middle East was the perceived need to conserve the mortal remains of the deceased intact. As a consequence, embalming techniques were developed, initially in fairly rudimentary form in the Fourth Dynasty, and became more elaborate during a process of evolution that reached its height during the New Kingdom. Embalming continued to be practiced in simplified forms in the Late Period and in the Graeco-Roman Period.

The funeral rituals were always very complicated. During the New Kingdom, following embalming, the coffin was transported by the deceased's relations to the west bank of the Nile on a boat adorned with flowers, amid the laments of those present and the propitiatory prayers offered to Osiris and Anubis by the priests. The boat was followed by a fleet of other vessels carrying

friends, furnishings, and offerings. Having reached the west bank of the river (where the necropolises were located), the sarcophagus was placed on a wagon drawn by oxen and a funeral procession formed along the route to the tomb. Here the ceremony of the "opening of the mouth and of the eyes" was performed to allow the deceased to regain the ability to speak, see, and feed himself in next world. The sarcophagus, the furnishings, and the offerings were then placed in the tomb before it was sealed for all eternity.

35
Detail of a wall painting in the burial chamber of the tomb of Tutankhamun in the Valley of the Kings. The scene depicts the ceremony of the opening of the mouth.

Hieroglyphic Writing

The deciphering of the hieroglyphs was the work of a young French scholar, Jean François Champollion, who in 1808 began to work on the so-called Rosetta Stone, the tri-lingual inscription in hieroglyphs, demotic, and Greek characters, found in 1799 by the Napoleonic troops near the town of Rosetta in the Nile delta.

Born in 1790, Champollion soon devoted himself to linguistic and Oriental studies and his deep knowledge of numerous idioms, above all Coptic, was of great help to him in the study and

unraveling of the secrets of hieroglyphic writing.

Appointed as a University of Grenoble professor at just nineteen years of age, Champollion devoted 14 years to the study of ancient Egyptian writing, basing his work on three remarkable intuitions: that Coptic constituted the ultimate development of Egyptian, that the hieroglyphs had a combined ideographic and phonetic meaning, and lastly, that the hieroglyphs enclosed within the cartouches transcribed phonetically the names of the pharaohs. Supposing that each hieroglyphic sign corresponded

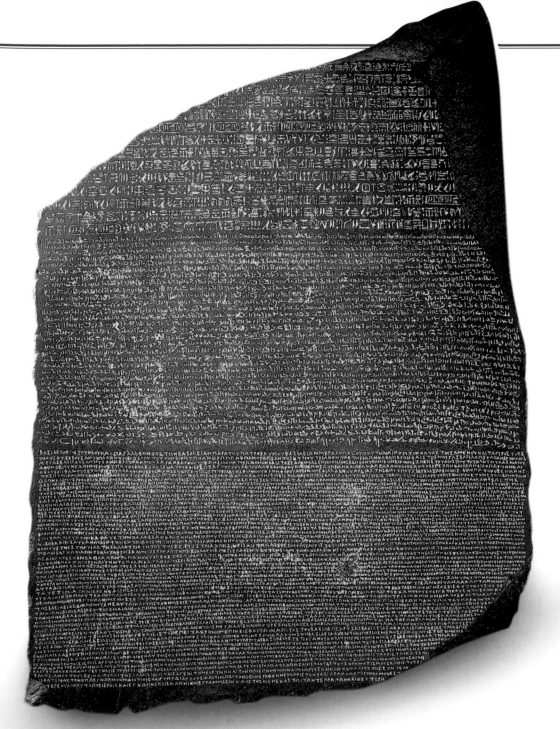

to a letter of the alphabet and knowing from the Greek text of the Rosetta Stone that the king it referred to was Ptolemy, he managed to identify the symbols that formed the name PTOLMYS.

Later, in 1821, by analyzing the bilingual text (Greek and hieroglyphs) on an obelisk discovered by Belzoni in the island of Philae and taken to England, he managed to decipher the name of Cleopatra and thus identify the alphabetical equivalent of no less than 12 symbols. Extending this methodology to other cartouches, Champollion discovered the equivalents of many hieroglyphs. In 1822 he presented his discovery to the academic world in the celebrated *Lettre à M. Dacier*, the secretary of the *Académie des Inscriptions et Belles Lettres*.

This was followed in 1824 by a book titled, *Précis du système hiéroglyphique des Anciens Egyptiens*, in which he explained the fundamental concepts of hieroglyphic writing. After having studied the inscriptions on numerous relics conserved in the European collections, Champollion, with the support of the King of France, Charles X, and the Grand Duke Leopold II of Tuscany, and accompanied by his most able disciple, Ippolito Rosellini, organized the Franco-Tuscan expedition that left Toulon for Egypt in July, 1828. Having finally reached the land of the pharaohs, Jean François Champollion was able to confirm his discoveries in the field, giving voice again to the language of ancient Egypt and founding a new discipline, Egyptology.

38 top left
The god Thot, protector of the scribes. Drawing taken from Ippolito Rosellini's Religious Monuments.

38 center right
Cartouches with the two names of the pharaoh Horemheb, taken from his tomb in the Valley of the Kings.

38 bottom
Scribe's palette in ivory from the tomb of Tutankhamun.

39 top center
Casket for brushes in gilded wood, part of the funerary cache of Tutankhamun.

39 left
Ivory papyrus burnisher, from the funerary cache of Tutankhamun.

39 top right
Scribe's palette in gilded wood, from the tomb of Tutankhamun.

39 bottom
Statue of a scribe in painted
limestone, from Saqqara.
5th Dynasty.

Travelers and
— Explorers —

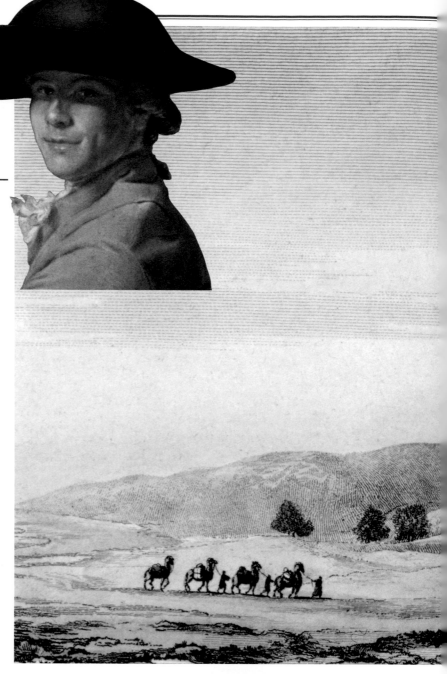

Following the publication of *Description de l'Egypte*
and the writings of Champollion, there was a veritable
race to Egypt on the part of academics, antiquarians,
adventurers, traffickers, the merely curious, and expert
Egyptologists. Even in antiquity, travelers of greater
or lesser fame had left traces of their passing: Homer,
Hecataeus of Miletus, Herodotus, Diodorus Siculus,
Strabo, Plutarch, and Plinius all visited Egypt.

The Roman emperors were by no means immune
to the appeal of Egypt and many commissioned
monuments such as the temple of Dendur by
Octavian Augustus or the Trajan pavillion at Philae,
or had their names inscribed on the existing
monuments.

Then, for long centuries, Egypt and its
monuments plunged into oblivion. Travelers and
merchants, in particular the Venetians, frequented the
country through their trading links with the East, but
never penetrated further into the country than Cairo.
Only in 1589 did an unknown merchant, the so-
called "Anonymous Venetian," ascend the Nile as far
as Thebes and write the earliest account since
antiquity of a trip to Upper Egypt to have survived.

Other travelers were to visit the country sporadically over the next two centuries (including the German Jesuit Kircher, the Frenchmen Sicard, Volney, and D'Anville, and the Englishmen James Bruce and Henry Salt), but we have to wait for the great expedition led by Napoleon for the first true study of the monuments of Egypt supported by drawings and maps. In 1798, Dominique Vivant Denon and the scholars enrolled by Napoleon to accompany his army explored Egypt, drawing, cataloging, and recording everything they found. The results of these labors were subsequently published in the *Déscription de l'Egypte*, a work of no less than nine volumes of text and eleven of folio-size plates, comprising three thousand drawings prepared by two hundred artists. The monuments of ancient Egypt, despite being covered with inscriptions, remained mute as far as the European travelers were concerned. In spite of the many attempts that were made, there was no way to decipher the writings of the pharaohs. In 1799, when the Napoleonic adventure was drawing to a close, a certain Lieutenant Bouchard casually discovered near the town of Rosetta in the Nile delta a stela that some years later was to prove to be the essential key to the hieroglyphs.

In the meantime, lots of discoveries were made: in 1813, the great Swiss orientalist, Johann Ludwig Burckhardt, brought to

42 top
The pasha Mohammed Ali, the undisputed ruler of Egypt from 1805 to 1849.

42 bottom
Bernardino Drovetti (1776-1852), French consul, posing before a colossal head at Thebes in 1818.

43 top left
Portrait in eastern garb of the traveler, Egyptologist, and adventurer, Giovanni Battista Belzoni (1778-1823).

43 top right
The artist, traveler, and diplomat Henry Salt was appointed British consul general to Egypt in 1816.

43 center
The recovery of a colossal bust of Rameses II at Thebes, directed by Belzoni in 1816.

43 bottom left
An enormous anthropoid sarcophagus, discovered by Heinrich von Minutoli in 1820.

light the temple of Abu Simbel while, after landing in Egypt in 1815, Giovanni Battista Belzoni of Padua was alone responsible for an extraordinary series of accomplishments between 1816 and 1818, including the opening of the great temple of Abu Simbel and the discoveries of the tomb of Sety I in the Valley of the Kings and the main entrance to the Pyramid of Khafre at Giza. Belzoni, a giant of a man and a dashing adventurer, was distinguished by his profound and sincere admiration for art and was, moreover, blessed with an unusual archaeological intuition and a remarkable capacity for solving numerous unforeseen technical problems.

In 1820, another Italian, Girolamo Segato, discovered the entrance to the stepped pyramid of Djoser and mapped vast areas of Upper Egypt and Nubia, reaching as far as the distant Siwa oasis.

In 1828, the young French scholar, Jean François Champollion, together with his pupil Ippolito Rosselini, organized the Franco-Tuscan expedition to verify in the field the validity of his deductions and to tackle new epigraphic documents. It was out of Champollion's remarkable intuitions that the modern discipline of Egyptology was born.

44 top left
*The Pisan Egyptologist,
Ippolito Rosellini (1800-
1843), the author of* The
Monuments of Egypt
and Nubia.

44 bottom left
*Rameses II in the act of
massacring a number of
enemies of various races.
Drawing taken from
Ippolito Rosellini's*
Historical Monuments.

A. Rosellini

During his stay in the land of the pharaohs, Rosellini
not only co-ordinated the execution of numerous
epigraphic surveys and drawings of the principal
monuments of ancient Egypt, but also acquired
important archaeological relics that now form the
nucleus of the Egyptian collection in Florence's
Museum of Archaeology. On his return to Italy he
published, between 1832 and 1844, the material
collected in his *Monumenti dell'Egitto e della Nubia*
(Monuments of Egypt and Nubia) from which the
illustrations on these pages are taken.

After his premature death, Champollion's work
was continued by the Prussian, Richard Lepsius, who
in 1842, organized an expedition which followed the
Nile as far as Meroe. He returned to Germany in
1848 and subsequently published his fundamental
work, *Denkmäler aus Ägypten und Äthiopien*, dedicated to

44-45
Rameses II aboard a war chariot, bas-relief in the hypostyle hall of the temple of Abu Simbel. Drawing taken from Ippolito Rosellini's Historical Monuments.

45 top right
Portrait of the Egyptologist Karl Richard Lepsius (1810-1884).

45 bottom right
The great temple of Abu Simbel, reproduced in Monuments of Egypt and Nubia, *published between 1849 and 1859 by Karl Richard Lepsius.*

the monuments of Egypt and Ethiopia.

Among the artists of the nineteenth century who depicted the splendors of the ancient kingdom of the pharaohs, mention should be made of Emile Prisse d'Avennes and David Roberts. Prisse d'Avennes (1807-1879), an engineer and architect of French origin, arrived in Egypt in 1827 at the invitation of the pasha, Mohammed Ali. Blessed with an agile and brilliant intellect, as well as a notable talent as a draftsman, and driven by a great curiosity regarding the remains of the past, he soon began to study the pharaonic monuments, without ignoring the various examples of Islamic art present in the country.

In 1836, Prisse d'Avennes ascended the Nile as far as Abu Simbel and subsequently resided at Luxor. After leaving the Nile valley

46
Rameses III from his tomb in the Valley of the Kings. Drawing by E.P. d'Avennes.

47 top left
The royal nurse holding the young Amenhotep II in her arms. By E.P. d'Avennes.

47 bottom left
A maid playing a lute in a bas-relief from the Theban tomb of Kenamun. Drawing by E.P. d'Avennes.

47 top right
Portrait of the Egyptologist and adventurer, Emile Prisse d'Avennes (1807-1879), in eastern clothes.

47 bottom right
The representatives of some foreign peoples paying homage to Amenhotep IV. Sketch by E.P. d'Avennes.

49 bottom
*The arrival of the Simun
at Giza.*

50-51
View of the temple of Philae.

*The five lithographs shown
are taken from Egypt and
Nubia (1846–1849) by
David Roberts.*

in 1844, he returned to France where he commenced publication of his drawings. Back in Egypt between 1858 and 1860, he devoted the rest of his life to the compilation of two works, the *Atlas de l'histoire de l'art égyptien* and *L'Art arabe d'apres le monuments du Caire*, the illustrations from which are still highly appreciated.

The Scotsman David Roberts (1796-1864), one of the most celebrated landscape painters of the nineteenth century, traveled to Egypt in 1838 and took the opportunity to depict all the principal archaeological sites and the mosques of Cairo. The superb lithographs produced from his drawings, published for the first time in London between 1846 and 1849 under the title *Egypt and Nubia*, document the state of preservation of the Egyptian monuments in the nineteenth century and provide valuable evidence of the colors of many bas-reliefs which have today been almost completely lost. It should also be remembered that the documentary work performed by Roberts took on particular significance with regards to the Nubian temples that, following the construction of the great Aswan Dam, inaugurated on January 15, 1971, had to be dismantled and rebuilt, frequently many miles away from their original sites.

Unfortunately, many of the landscapes drawn by the artist have been lost forever.

David Roberts R.A.   L. Haghe lith.

Grand Portico of the Temple of Philae — Nubia

The Birth of Modern Archaeology

52 top left
Portrait of Gaston Maspéro (1846-1916), director of the Service des Antiquités Egyptiennes.

52 bottom left
A phase of Jacques de Morgan's recovery of the statues concealed in the "cachette" at Karnak in 1903.

52 center
Portrait of Auguste Mariette (1821-1881), creator of the Service des Antiquités Egyptiennes and founder of the Egyptian Museum of Cairo.

52 right
Portrait of the Egyptologist, Ernesto Schiaparelli (1856-1928), director of the Egyptian Museum of Turin.

53
The Valley of the Kings, November, 1922: Howard Carter and Arthur Callender open the doors of the four gilded wooden shrines containing the sarcophagi of Tutankhamun.

In 1850, a modest employee at the Louvre arrived in Egypt charged with the acquisition of Coptic manuscripts. This was Auguste Mariette. An acute observer and an expert on ancient texts, on his own initiative he organized digs at Memphis, between Saqqara and Abu-sir, thus bringing to light the Serapeum, the necropolis where the divine Apis bulls were worshipped. This important archaeological discovery— to be followed by that of the lower temple of the Pyramid of Khafre—brought fame to the unknown clerk and in 1858 he was appointed by the Viceroy Said Pasha as conservator of monuments with extensive powers. He was responsible for the creation of the Museum of Cairo and, on his death in 1882, he was buried in the museum courtyard.

Mariette's successor was Gaston Maspèro who undertook important excavations at Giza and Luxor. He was also responsible for the discovery of the famous "cachette" of Deir al-Bahari where the mummies of a number of pharaohs from the Eighteenth and Nineteenth Dynasties were concealed (Amenhotep I, Rameses I and II, and Sety I).

Between the end of the nineteenth and the beginning of the twentieth centuries, archaeological campaigns followed one another in rapid succession, but were now regulated by legislation that required

54-55
Howard Carter
photographed while cleaning
the solid gold third coffin of
Tutankhamun.

54 bottom left
The treasure chamber, in the
tomb of Tutankhamun,
dominated by the fearsome
statue of Anubis.

54 bottom right
Arthur Mace and Alfred
Lucas, assistants to Howard
Carter, intent on the
restoration of one of the
guardian statues discovered
within the tomb of
Tutankhamun.

fair division of relics found between the countries financing the digs and the Egyptian government. Among the most well known financiers was the British aristocrat, George Edward Stanhope Molyneux Herbert, Earl of Carnarvon, who spent much time in Egypt for health reasons. Here Carnarvon met a young English archaeologist, Howard Carter (born in 1874), and commissioned him to undertake excavations on his behalf. After various digs, in 1914 Carnarvon obtained permission to work in the Valley of the Kings, an area that most experts considered to be archaeologically exhausted. On examining a number of clues, Carter was convinced that the valley contained an unknown tomb that ought to belong to the pharaoh Tutankhamun, a name that had been found on a stela discovered in the temple of Karnak and on a number of relics found in the valley itself. The outbreak of the First World War obliged Carter to postpone his search until 1917. Excavations went on with no great results till 1921. Lord Carnarvon, who had invested significant sums, was on the point of abandoning the enterprise and suspending his financial support, but allowed Carter to make one last attempt.

Work began in the autumn of 1922. On the fourth of November, one of the workers found a stone step, the first of a flight that descended into the rock. Carter, perhaps intuiting the long-awaited discovery, covered the find and telegraphed Carnarvon in England, asking him to come to the site immediately. Work recommenced on the twenty-fourth of November and the staircase was soon cleared of detritus and the two Englishmen found themselves before a sealed doorway, followed by a second internal door. Both carried the seals of the necropolis and the name of Tutankhamun. On November 26, Carter, Carnarvon and his daughter Evelyn, and the archaeologist Callender, who had recently joined the dig, could finally make a hole in the second door and observe the interior of the tomb and the treasures it contained. This was the first and to date, the only royal tomb to be found practically intact in the history of Egyptology, even though study of the remains revealed that in antiquity it had already been the object of two violations, fortunately without serious consequences.

The emptying of the tomb of Tutankhamun took years with around 3,500 objects being recovered, including the famous solid gold sarcophagus weighing over 240 pounds, confirming that this was the most

55 top
Lord Carnarvon, financier of the dig that led to the discovery of the tomb of Tutankhamun, photographed at Thebes in 1924.

55 bottom
The antechamber of the tomb of Tutankhamun at the moment of discovery, with the pharaoh's dismantled war chariots and the ritual beds.

exceptional archaeological find ever made in Egypt.

In 1939, the French archaeologist Pierre Montet, who was conducting a dig in the eastern region of the delta at San al-Haggar, the site of the ancient city of Tanis, discovered the inviolate tombs of the pharaohs of the Twenty-first and Twenty-second Dynasties. The magnificent funerary cache found in the tomb of the pharaoh Psusennes, composed of jewels, gold and silver vases, and gold masks, reveals remarkable artistry. Alongside the tomb of the sovereign, Montet discovered a further four belonging to Psusennes' successor, Amenemophis, the general Undjebaunded, Osorkon II, and the pharaoh Sheshonq II. The discovery of the royal necropolis of Tanis and its treasures closed an era in the history of Egyptology which had begun with the discoveries of Belzoni and continued with that of Carter. However, Egypt has continued to reserve surprises for researchers. Finds of great importance have in fact continued up to the present day.

In 1989 an extremely interesting cachette (a hiding place) was found within the Temple of Luxor that contained statues in perfect condition dating from the New Kingdom. They can today be seen in the Museum of Luxor's new gallery. The discovery that has aroused much interest around the world has been, however, that of a necropolis from the Roman Period from between the first and second centuries A.D., in the Bahariya oasis.

56-57
The discovery of a number of statues buried in the courtyard of Amenhotep III at Luxor early in 1989.

56 bottom left
The discovery of the pyramid of Queen Ankherespepy II, near Saqqara.

56 bottom right
A French archaeologist copying a hieroglyphic text in the pyramid of Pepy I.

In 1996, a donkey's hoof sank into the sand and the small hole produced revealed the existence of a subterranean tomb. In the months that followed, the excavations directed by the celebrated Egyptian archaeologist Zahi Hawass brought to light around a hundred mummies wrapped in gilded cartonnage. For this reason the necropolis is now known as the "Valley of the Golden Mummies." As the area is very extensive, the exerts believe that in the future over 10,000 may be found and that the excavation work could last for decades. Another very recent discovery is that of the intact tomb of the plenipotentiary governor of the Bahariya oasis who lived during Twenty-sixth Dynasty (around 500 B.C., prior to the conquest of Egypt by the Persian Cambyses) when the oasis was at the height of its economic development. The tomb was found to contain a limestone sarcophagus with hieroglyphic inscriptions and a cache comprising amulets in gold and faience. Lastly, at Alexandria, the Frenchman, Frank Goddio, an expert in submarine archaeology, has brought to light numerous relics and identified the submerged island of Antìrrodos where Cleopatra had a palace.

57 top
The famous Egyptian archaeologist, Zahi Hawas cleaning some of the mummies from the oasis of Bahariya. This location has become famous as the "Valley of the Golden Mummies."

57 bottom
In 1995, in the waters off the port of Alexandria, a team led by the French archaeologist, Frank Goddio, discovered numerous monumental remains, statues, and sculptural fragments, perhaps belonging to one of Queen Cleopatra's palaces and the celebrated Lighthouse.

—— Archeological Itineraries ——

Alexandria

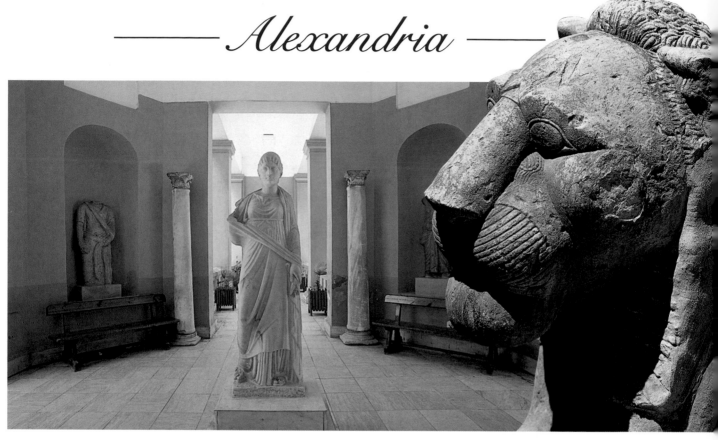

K nown in Arabic as Al-Iskandariya, Alexandria is situated in the extreme north of Egypt, on the strip of land separating the Mediterranean from Lake Mariyut. It was founded by Alexander the Great in 332-331 B.C., on the site of the Egyptian town of Rhakotis. The great Macedonian conqueror intended to provide Egypt with a new capital and Mediterranean Greece and the East with a port, preferring this option to the destroyed Tyre due to its more central position which made it a potential center for trade in the Mediterranean. It is not known whether Alexander intended the city to be one of the metropolises of the universal empire he dreamed of, but the site soon proved to be well chosen. However, he did not stay there long enough to see a single building completed.

Following his mysterious visit to the priest of the temple of Jupiter-Amun in the Siwa oasis, Alexander departed to devote himself to the conquest of Asia. Eight years later, he died prematurely at 33 years of age. His body was embalmed and placed in a tomb in Alexandria with all the honors and funerary rituals normally accorded to a pharaoh.

One of Alexander the Great's generals, Ptolemy, promptly took up the reins of power and installed a new dynasty destined to endure for around three centuries until Cleopatra VII's suicide in 30 B.C.

Under the aegis of the Ptolemaic Dynasty, Alexandria became a flourishing, cosmopolitan city, the largest in the ancient world before Rome imposed its supremacy, thanks to extensive trading with the peoples of the Mediterranean. The union of the Greek and Egyptian cultures meant that to all intents and purposes the city also became the cultural center of the country. Thanks to thinkers and scientists such as Euclid, Aristarchus of Samos, Eratosthenes, Herophilus, and Eratistratus, it was also the cradle of methodological criticism and philology, classical geometry and astronomy, map-making, the medicine of the central nervous system and the circulation of blood. Classical literature mentions two extraordinary institutions of learning and scientific research, the Library and the Museum. Unfortunately nothing now remains of either, nor of the Pharos lighthouse, considered to be one of the Seven Wonders of the World. A

60 top
The fortress of Qaitbey, erected in the 15th century on the foundations of the famous lighthouse of Alexandria.

60 bottom left
A view of the Museum of Graeco-Roman Antiquities which conserves remains from the period 300 B.C. to 300 A.D.

60 bottom right
A detail of a sandstone lion conserved in the Museum of Graeco-Roman Antiquities.

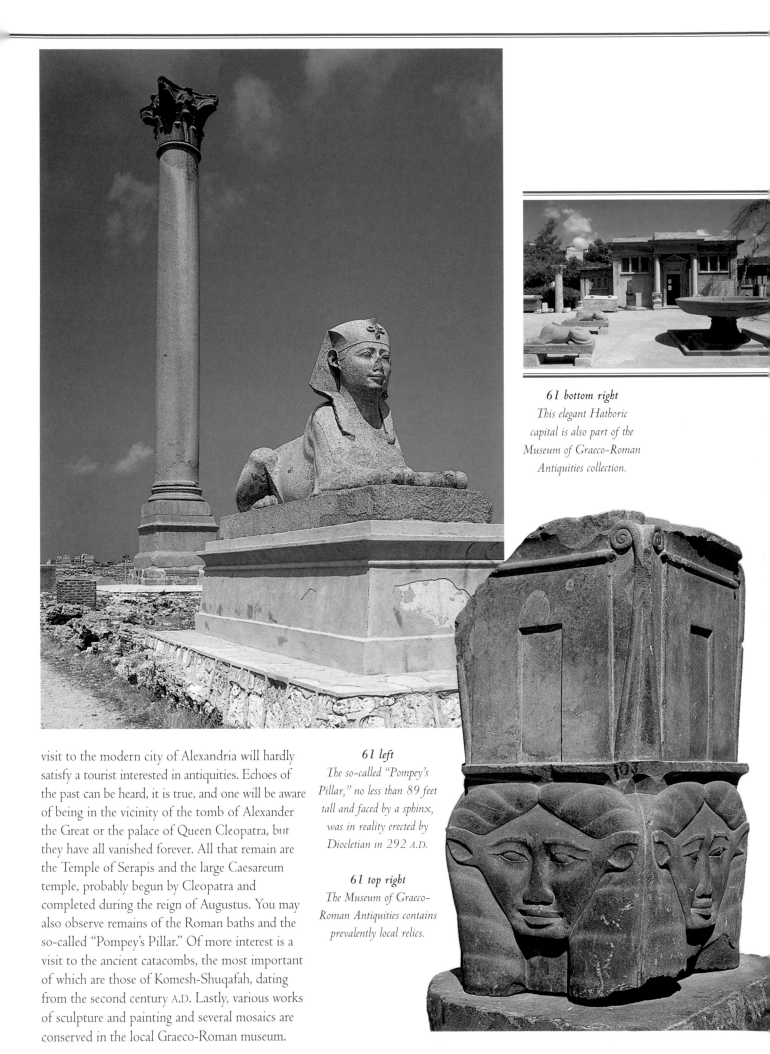

visit to the modern city of Alexandria will hardly satisfy a tourist interested in antiquities. Echoes of the past can be heard, it is true, and one will be aware of being in the vicinity of the tomb of Alexander the Great or the palace of Queen Cleopatra, but they have all vanished forever. All that remain are the Temple of Serapis and the large Caesareum temple, probably begun by Cleopatra and completed during the reign of Augustus. You may also observe remains of the Roman baths and the so-called "Pompey's Pillar." Of more interest is a visit to the ancient catacombs, the most important of which are those of Komesh-Shuqafah, dating from the second century A.D. Lastly, various works of sculpture and painting and several mosaics are conserved in the local Graeco-Roman museum.

61 bottom right
This elegant Hathoric capital is also part of the Museum of Graeco-Roman Antiquities collection.

61 left
The so-called "Pompey's Pillar," no less than 89 feet tall and faced by a sphinx, was in reality erected by Diocletian in 292 A.D.

61 top right
The Museum of Graeco-Roman Antiquities contains prevalently local relics.

61

Tanis

62 top and center

Among the remains of the Great Temple of Tanis, of particular note are the fragments of two sandstone colossal statues of Rameses II.

62 bottom

The tip of one of the obelisks that adorned the Great Temple of Amun.

Tanis (Za'net in Egyptian), the capital of the Fourteenth Nome of Lower Egypt, is situated on the eastern side of the Nile delta, around 81 miles north-east of Cairo and 31 from the Mediterranean. The first survey of the site was made by the Napoleonic expedition, while the Frenchman Rifaud completed the first systematic excavations in 1825 and found the two large, pink granite sphinxes now conserved in the Louvre. Since then, archaeological work has continued almost uninterruptedly, directed by eminent Egyptologists such as Mariette, Petrie, P. Montet, and J. Yoyotte. These excavations have mainly brought to light relics from the Twenty-first Dynasty through to the Ptolemaic Period.

The casual discovery of relics from the Ramesside epoch and earlier periods prompted suggestions that this may have been the biblical city of Pi-Rameses, built by the Jews and their point of departure towards the promised land. The enigma has in part been resolved. It now appears certain that the stones of earlier times were transported to the sites in question for successive rebuilding work, a common practice among the ancient Egyptians. The site's principal feature is the remains of the great temple of Amun, protected by a rectangular enclosure wall of brick measuring 1,411 x 1,214 feet within which — and in part integral with — is a second, the bricks of which are inscribed with the name of the pharaoh Psusennes I of the Twenty-first dynasty.

At the center of the enclosure stood the great Temple of Amun, now reduced to an expanse of columns, obelisks, and statues of different eras with inscriptions and decorative motifs generally dating back to Rameses II. To the north of the temple is a sacred lake while to the east are the ruins of a granite temple. The Temple of Mut and Khonsus, also known as the Temple of Anta, stands outside the brick curtain walls.

In 1866, the German Egyptologist, Karl

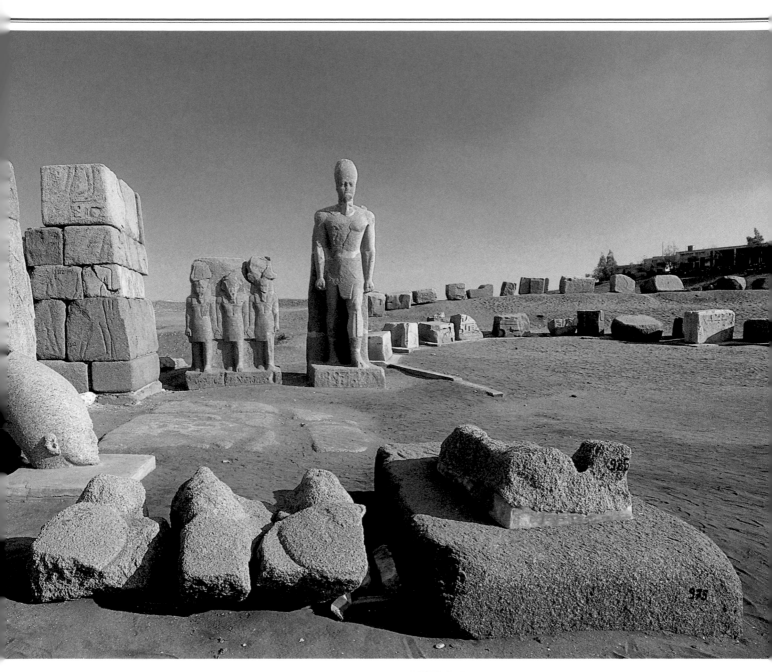

Lepsius, discovered a block of stone at Tanis that has become known as the Canopus Decree (comparable in importance to Egyptology to the Rosetta stone). On one side it carries a hieroglyphic inscription and its Greek translation, and on the other the same text in demotic characters.

In 1939, the French Egyptologist, Montet, made a discovery second in importance only to that of the tomb of Tutankhamun: a subterranean necropolis with the intact royal tombs of Psusennes I, Osorkon II, and Sheshonq III (Twenty-first–Twenty-second Dynasties). The precious finds, silver sarcophaghi, gold masks, and jewels are now exhibited in the Egyptian Museum of Cairo.

64 left
The solid gold funerary
mask of Psusennes I,
discovered at Tanis by
Pierre Montet.

64 bottom right
Gold and lapis lazuli
pectoral of Sheshonq II,
found at Tanis.

65 top
Pendant in the form of a winged scarab, in gold and semiprecious stones, part of the funerary goods of Psusenne I.

64-65 top
Gold collar, found in the tomb of Psusennes I at Tanis.

64-65 center
The sarcophagus of Psusennes I was made of solid silver, a metal the Egyptians considered to be more precious than gold.

65 bottom
Gold, lapis lazuli, and vitreous enamel pectoral found in the tomb of Sheshonq II at Tanis.

—Giza's Plateau—

66 center
The Pyramid of Khufu and, in the foreground, the mastabas of the necropolis.

66 bottom
The pyramids of Giza, perfectly aligned from north-east to south-west.

66 top
The Sphinx and the Pyramid of Khufu cloaked in the dawn mists.

Located around 7 miles from Cairo, the Giza Plateau extends on the edge of the Western Desert. The flat, regular conformation of the plateau made it an ideal site for the construction of monuments, while its position to the west of the Nile, that is to say, towards the setting sun, was a religious prerequisite for necropolises. The vicinity of the river also facilitated the transportation of materials.

A bed of nummulite fossils (foraminiferous protozoa common in the warm seas following the Jurassic period, around 100,000,000 years ago) dating from the late Cretaceous, early Tertiary period has been discovered to the north-west of the plateau.

The slope extends towards the south-east with alternate strata of hard and soft rock. In this area the ancient Egyptians removed the softer limestone to reach the harder strata which they cut up into blocks to use for the construction of pyramids, tombs, and temples.

Towards the south rises an irregular relief feature (Maadi) characterized by numerous chasms, *wadis* (dry river beds), and gorges from which the stones and clay needed for building were extracted.

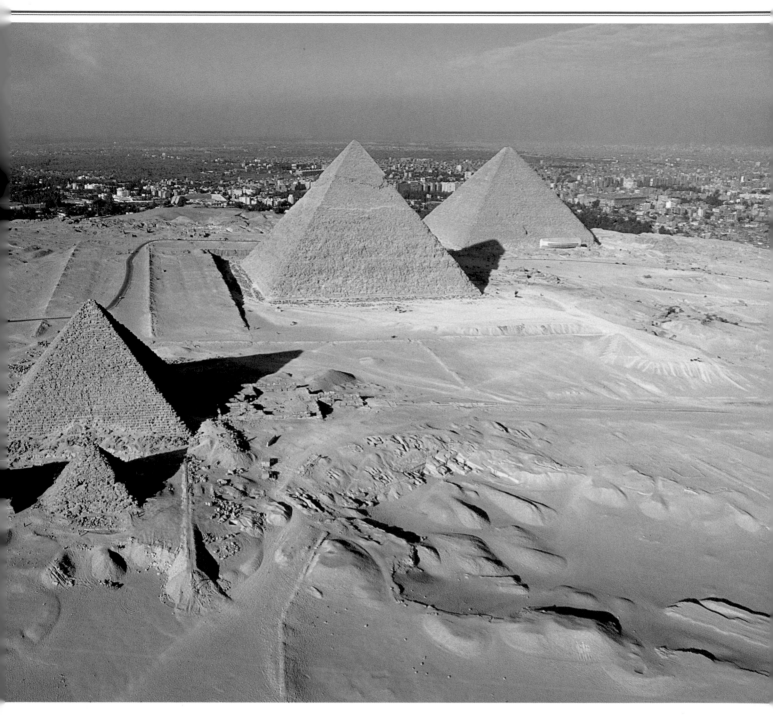

These were materials of good quality, easily extracted and close to the building sites.

The white limestone used for the outer covering of the pyramids came from Tura, on the east bank of the Nile, while the granite arrived by river from Aswan (as testified by the bas-reliefs in the Fifth Dynasty pyramid of Unas in nearby Saqqara).

What is perhaps the oldest tomb on the plateau was discovered by an Italian, Barsanti, in 1904, around 3 miles from the pyramid of Khufu, while a little higher is a mastaba from the Second Dynasty. Already considered sacred before the construction of the great pyramids, this area was called Kheret-Neter-Akhet-Khufu (Necropolis of the Horizon of Khufu). It was also known as Rostaw, a reference to the legend whereby Osiris was the god of the dead and "Lord of Rostaw," or the sovereign of the caverns and passages thought to lie beneath the Giza plateau. In the light of recent excavations conducted by Zahi Hawass, the existence of such passages is more plausible today.

The plateau is, of course dominated by the three great pyramids and the Sphinx.

66-67

A panoramic view of the archaeological area of Giza: in the foreground rises the Pyramid of Menkaura.

68 bottom right
*The burial chamber of
Khafre, discovered by
Giovanni Battista Belzoni
in 1818.*

69
*The narrow corridor that
leads to the burial chamber
in the Pyramid of Khufu.*

THE PYRAMIDS

68-69
*An unusual view of the
Pyramid of Khufu.*

68 bottom left
*The solar boat, discovered in
1954 in a trench at the
foot of the Pyramid of
Khufu, is today conserved in
a custom-built museum.*

THE PYRAMID OF KHUFU

Built during the reign of Khufu between 2551 and 2528 B.C., the Great Pyramid was almost certainly conceived as a funerary monument for the pharaoh's burial. Little is known about Khufu's time and many hypotheses regarding the monument should be treated with caution.

Herodotus recounts that the pyramid was built over the course of 20 years, with 100,000 men working three-month shifts, figures that might not be far from reality. The pyramid form had a religious-symbolic significance associated with the representation in stone of solar rays or the primordial hill at the origins of the world.

Considered by the ancients to be one of the Seven Wonders of the World, the building still arouses admiration and awe, due both to its sheer bulk and the surprising precision of its dimensions given the instruments available 4,500 years ago.

The sides of the base measure 755.9 x 756.3 x 756.6 x 754.4 feet, the total difference of just 8 inches equating to a margin of error of one in a thousand. At 481 feet in height, the Great Pyramid was the world's tallest building until the construction of the Eiffel Tower in 1889. The volume of around 95,353,000 cubic feet is composed of around 2,500,000 blocks of stone weighing on average 5,500 pounds each.

The precision of the geographical alignment of the entrance face is equally surprising. The deviation from due north is just 0° 3' 6".

The present-day stepped appearance is due to the removal, during the period of Arab domination, of the external covering in white Tura limestone which would have made the pyramid glow brightly in the sun.

Today the summit is truncated, creating a platform, but in the past it would have terminated at 481 feet with a possibly gilded *pyramidion*. The entrance is situated on the north face at a height of about 49 feet. The current access, a passage created by ancient tomb robbers, is lower. A descending corridor leads to a subterranean chamber, while a rising passage instead leads to the Grand Gallery and the Queen's Chamber. The latter was not actually a female royal tomb, but was named as such by the Arab visitors due to its unusual double pitched ceiling.

The King's Chamber, the object of controversy and unresolved mystery, features walls dressed with monolithic blocks of granite, the same material also being used for the nine ceiling slabs. All of the granite elements are perfectly hewn and fit together with absolute precision. The monolithic sarcophagus, made of the same type of pink granite, lacks inscriptions and the cover is missing.

Outside the building, alongside the east face, are three satellite pyramids attributed to the queens Hetepheres, Meritetes, and Henutsen. On the south side of the pyramid, the Museum of the Solar Boat contains a perfectly restored and reassembled funerary boat over 130 feet long that would once have sailed on the Nile.

70-71
A view of the Pyramid of Khafre which reveals the limestone covering of the summit.

70 bottom left
The Pyramid of Khafre throws its shadow on that of Khufu, surrounded by the vast necropolis.

THE PYRAMID OF KHAFRE

While smaller than the Pyramid of Khufu (705 x 705 x 471 feet), the Pyramid of Khafre is nonetheless impressive as it is situated slightly higher than the other and its external covering has survived at the top below the tip.

The entrance is located on the north side and was discovered by Giovanni Belzoni in 1818. At the end of a long corridor is a single funerary chamber, excavated in the rock and featuring a ceiling of limestone slabs. A black granite sarcophagus with no inscriptions stands in the chamber.

THE PYRAMID OF MENKAURA

This is the smallest of the three (335.3 x 343.2 x 213 feet), but must have been extremely beautiful as it was once coated with pink granite.

The entrance is located at the base of the north side and leads, by way of a corridor, to a unfinished mortuary chamber excavated in the rock at a depth of around 20 feet. A second passage leads to the burial chamber. Here a basalt sarcophagus was discovered, lacking inscriptions but decorated with architectural motifs. Unfortunately the relic was lost in a shipwreck while being transported to Europe.

70 bottom right
A view of the Pyramid of Menkaura, with the three satellite pyramids.

71 top
Another view of the Pyramid of Khafre.

71 bottom
The tomb of Seshmnefer, a court dignitary from the late 4th Dynasty.

72-73
The construction of the
Sphinx is attributed to
Khafre, the pharaoh whose
facial features the colossus is
thought to represent.

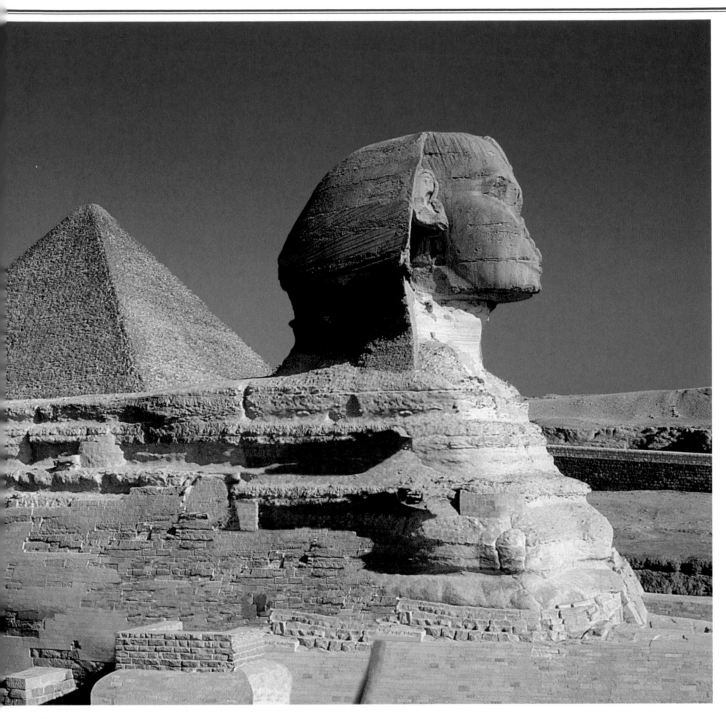

THE SPHINX

The Sphinx is located around 1640 feet east of the Pyramid of Khafre, along the monumental road that linked the funerary temple with the lower temple of the pharaoh. The monument was sculpted in the living limestone of the plateau, utilizing a protuberance in the terrain that was probably created by quarrying work.

The human head is wearing a *nemes* headcloth with an asp and the false beard of the pharaohs (relics found in the sand by G. Caviglia), while the body is that of a crouching lion, a symbol of regal power. The face of the pharaoh is thought to be that of Khafre himself.

Between the front paws stands the stela of Thutmosis IV, commemorating a premonitory dream of the pharaoh according to which he would have acceded to power had he excavated the sphinx which had on a number of occasions been buried by the sand. The scrupulous observer Herodotus perhaps did not mention the Sphinx because he could not actually see it. The ruins of the temple on which the sphinx rises (the Temple of the Sphinx) flank the Lower Temple of Khafre, the architecture of which features incredibly precise masonry with large granite blocks being used for columns, architraves, and internal coverings.

While on the Giza plateau one should also visit the (where accessible) Fourth and Fifth Dynasty mastabas around the Pyramid of Khufu.

74-75

The face of time: the nose of the sphinx is broken, the eyes riddled, and the beard detached from the chin. Erosion has revealed the original geological layers, but the hardness of the rock of the head still ensures that the pharaoh's splendid, divine majesty emerges.

— The Egyptian Museum in Cairo —

Those approaching the art and culture of ancient Egypt for the first time are faced with such a vast quantity of material that it is almost impossible to gain a complete overview. Visiting the Egyptian Museum in Cairo is thus indispensable for placing in context such a variety and abundance of archaeological marvels and for getting a more exhaustive picture of what the Egyptians were capable of from the dawn of the Bronze Age, around 4,500 years ago.

Created in 1858 by the Frenchman Auguste Mariette in river port buildings in the Bulaq quarter, the first collection of Egyptian antiquities was moved in 1902 to its present location close to the Midan al-Tahrir square, almost on the Nile banks. The building has not been subjected to significant modifications, something which cannot be said of the chaotic urban context in which it is set. Besieged by the city, the present-day museum is immersed in gardens containing dozens of sculptural works and the mausoleum of its founder who was reluctant to be separated from the magnificent collections even after his death.

The museum's over 100 rooms contain the world's largest collection of Egyptian antiquities, around 100,000 works, while the warehouses also contain tens of thousands of relics.

The two-tier exhibition criteria were established by Mariette himself: the ground floor is devoted to the great sculptural works, arranged chronologically, covering the history of Egypt from the Archaic and Protodynastic Periods through to the Late, Saitic, Persian, and Graeco-Roman Periods. The first floor instead features collections subdivided according to types of objects.

Visitors enter the Great Gallery on the ground floor which houses the stone sarcophagi of the Old Kingdom, and then encounter the statues of the great sovereigns from the era of the pyramids, between the Third and the Fourth Dynasties (from the limestone simulacrum of

76 top
Sphinx of Thutmosis III located outside the museum.

76 top center
An unusual view of the hall of the Egyptian Museum.

76 bottom center
One wing of the museum's Honor Gallery.

76 bottom
The summit of an obelisk of Rameses II, from Tanis, now located in the garden of the museum.

76-77
The façade of the Egyptian Museum, overlooking a garden adorned with relics

from throughout Egypt. Building work on the museum began in 1897 and it was opened in 1902.

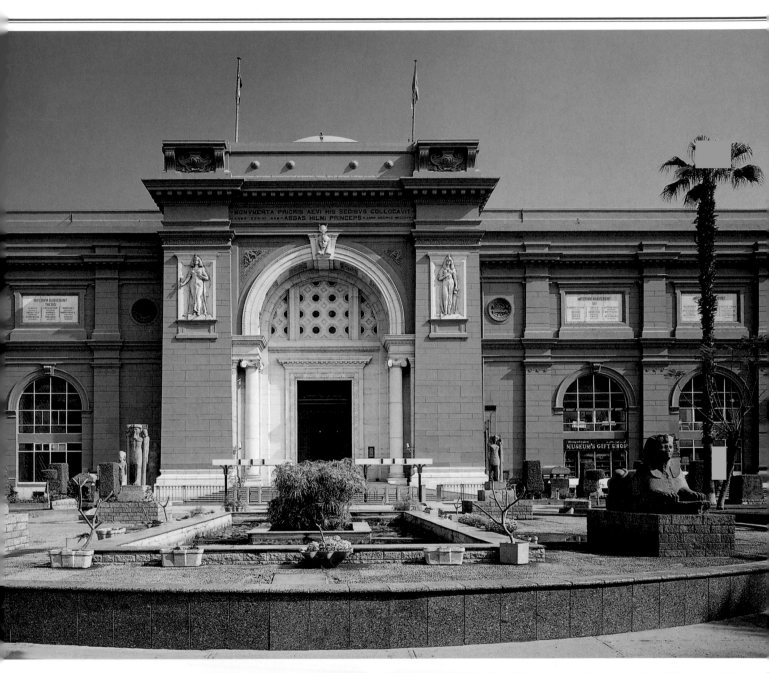

77 bottom left
A statue of a seated lion in pink granite, dating from the Late Period and discovered at Tell al-Muqdam. This piece is also located in the museum garden.

77 bottom right
The wide central room of the Egyptian Museum, surrounded by the other rooms where finds are displayed.

Djoser to the diorite statue of Khafre and the triads of Menkaura, in polished schist), and high ranking figures such as the multicolored sculptural group of the priest Rahotep, son of the Fourth Dynasty king, Snefru, and his wife Nefret, found at Meidum.

Gravitating around the colossal statue of Amenhotep III sitting alongside his wife Tiy that occupies the central corridor and proceeding in a clockwise direction through the ground floor rooms one finds statues and stelae relating to the sovereigns of the Middle Kingdom (Amememhat III and Senusret I), the New Kingdom (from the statue of Thutmosis III as a boy, to the sphinx with the features of Queen Hatshepsut, up to the four colossal statues of the heretical pharaoh Akhenaten, absolutely unique with respect to the traditional art of ancient Egypt), and the Late Period. There is also the fascinating funerary chamber of Harhotep, from Deir al-Bahari, featuring magnificent decorated furnishings.

The visit continues on the first floor where a separate ticket has to be purchased for the hall containing the mummies. The visitors' attention is generally concentrated on the recently restored halls containing the 2,099 relics of the Treasure of Tutankhamun, discovered by Howard Carter in the Valley of the Kings in 1922. Here the visitor is greeted by a succession of thrilling display cases

78-79
The Geese of Meidum,
painted on plaster.
4th Dynasty.

78 bottom left
A detail of the statue of
Nefret, from Meidum.
4th Dynasty.

78 bottom right
The Narmer Palette, bas-
relief on green schist, from
Hierakonpolis.
Dynasty 0.

79 top
Hippopotamus in blue
Faience, from the necropolis
of Dra Abu al-Naga.
Second Intermediate Period.

with, alongside the relics exhibited and published innumerable times throughout the world, hundreds of other fabulous objects that were intended to accompany the king on his journey to the Afterlife and now compose the richest and most complete funerary cache yet to be discovered in Egypt. In addition to the museum's 12 most popular rooms, the first floor also offers other funerary treasures of exceptional value, including the particularly interesting collection of Queen Hetepheres (mother of Khufu), examples of the goldsmiths' art that cover the history of Egypt from the primordial era through to the Byzantine era, and a body of hieroglyphic texts on papyrus taken from the *Book of the Dead*. This floor is also rich in relics that narrate something of the ordinary lives of the ancient Egyptians, models of armies and homes, tools and jewellery, "minor" objects that are nonetheless capable of captivating the interest of visitors even more than the majesty of the great statues and the dazzling gold.

79 bottom left
Triad of Menkaura, grey-green schist, from Giza.
4th Dynasty.

79 bottom right
Statue of Khafre, in diorite, found at Giza.
4th Dynasty.

80-81 top
*Model depicting the
livestock count from
Deir al-Bahari.
11th Dynasty.*

80-81 bottom
*Model depicting
a troop of Nubian archers,
from Assiut.
11th Dynasty.*

81
Model of a fishing scene on the Nile, from Deir al-Bahari. 12th Dynasty.

82
Upper part of a sandstone colossus statue representing Amenhotep IV, from Karnak. 18th Dynasty.

83
Unfinished head in quartzite of Queen Nefertiti, from Tell al-Amarna. 18th Dynasty.

84
Solid gold death mask of Tutankhamun, from the Valley of the Kings. 18th Dynasty.

85 top left
Simulacrum of the god Anubis, in tarred and gilded wood, from the Valley of the Kings. 18th Dynasty.

85 bottom left
Gilded wood statue of the ka of Tutankhamun, from the Valley of the Kings. 18th Dynasty.

85 right and 86-87
Tutankhamun's throne made from wood, gold leaf, precious stones, and glass paste; from the Valley of the Kings, 18th Dynasty.

88-89
Tutankhamon fires an arrow at wild birds; image taken from the statue sanctuary in the Valley of the Kings, 18th Dynasty.

90 top
Pendant in gold and semi-precious stones in the form of a falcon, from the tomb of Tutankhamun, Valley of the Kings. 18th Dynasty.

90 bottom
Container for canopic jars in alabaster, from the tomb of Tutankhamun in the Valley of the Kings. 18th Dynasty.

92-93
Pectoral with Tutankhamun's first name in a winged scarab; from the Valley of the Kings, 18th Dynasty.

90-91
Internal coffin in solid gold, semi-precious stones and vitreous enamel, that contained the mummy of

Tutankhamun. This extraordinary piece weighs 243.4 pounds. From the Valley of the Kings. 18th Dynasty.

91 top
Shrine in gilded wood for the canopic jars of Tutankhamun, from the Valley of the Kings. 18th Dynasty.

94 left
Wooden sarcophagus of
Rameses II, from the Valley
of the Kings.
19th Dynasty.

94 top right
Portrait of a young woman,
tempera on wood, from
al-Rubayat.
Roman Period.

94 bottom right
Colossal statue in granite
and limestone of the young
Rameses II and the god
Horus, from Tanis.
19th Dynasty.

95
Portrait of two brothers,
encaustic on wood,
from Antaeopolis.
Roman Period.

96-97 and 96 bottom
Limestone colossal statue of Rameses II, 33.8 feet tall. Now conserved in a custom-built modern construction.

Memphis

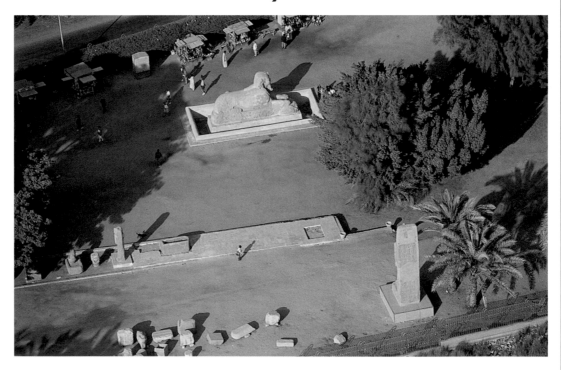

97 top
This great alabaster sphinx is no less than 26 feet long and weighs 8 tons.

97 bottom
Aerial view of the local open-air museum, with the alabaster sphinx.

The few ruins of Memphis, the capital of the Old Kingdom, are located around 19 miles from Cairo, near the village of Al-Badrashein, and not far from the necropolis of Saqqara South. Tradition has it that Memphis was founded by Menes, or Aha, the first king of the First Dynasty. For centuries Memphis was the sole capital of Egypt until, at the beginning of the New Kingdom, it was joined by Thebes in the administrative and spiritual leadership of the country. An important religious center during the Ptolemaic Period, Memphis began to decline in the face of the cultural rise of Alexandria and during the Mameluke dominion it was neglected to the point where it was flooded by the Nile.

Today, visitors can admire, in particular, the prostrate colossal statue of Rameses II sculpted from a single block of calcareous stone and originally 46 feet high and an alabaster Sphinx, with the features of Amenhotep II, opposite the temple of Ptah.

─── *Saqqara* ───

Not far from the archaeological area of Memphis, in a westerly direction, lies the necropolis of Saqqara South. The northern part of the area comprises the pryramids of Djedkara Isesi, the Fifth Dynasty ruler, and of Pepy I and Merenra, both Sixth Dynasty sovereigns. The first is the best preserved, but all have lost the interior decoration that featured the sacred Pyramid Texts. These are instead legible in the pyramid of Pepy II, located a short distance to the south. Nearby, the al-Farun mastaba is the tomb of Shepseskaf, last king of the Fourth Dynasty. The two-stepped monument has the rectangular form of a a sarcophagus and is oriented east-west.

Heading north towards Giza you will reach the principal archaeological site of Saqqara housing one of the oldest pharaonic necropolises in Egypt. Like Giza, the complex stands on a plateau raised above the level of the Nile.

Excavations began in 1912, bringing to light in the northern area tombs and mastabas from the First Dynasty. The mastaba attributed to Aha was found to contain objects, weapons, and the oldest papyrus ever to be discovered.

THE FUNERARY COMPLEX OF DJOSER

The funerary complex of Djoser is the most important monumental work at Saqqara and was built by the vizier Imhotep, an architect and court physician. The oldest of the Egyptian pyramids is enclosed within a rectangular limestone wall, originally decorated with pilasters and 14 false doors on each face. The very narrow entrance leads into a gallery with 40 clustered pillars arranged in two rows.

The base of the six-stepped pyramid is rectangular and the terraced summit tops out at 192,9 feet. The pyramid was built in five phases, departing from an initial mastaba tomb.

98 top
Aerial view of the necropolis of Saqqara, the largest in Egypt.

98 center
The remains of the so-called "royal pavilion" in the Djoser complex.

98 bottom
The entrance opened in the curtain wall surrounding the Djoser complex.

98-99 and 99 bottom
The pyramid of Djoser is the fruit of five successive enlargements of a mastaba.

100-101
The Step Pyramid dominates the archaeological site of North Saqqara.

The interior is very complex. The funerary chamber of Djoser is at the bottom of a shaft almost in the center of the building, while the subterranean sections develop in a labyrinth of corridors, staircases, shafts, and chambers over 3 miles long.

The stores contained shards of over 40,000 vases, 4,000 of which have been reconstructed, as well as jugs, plates, trays, and sarcophaghi, all funerary furnishings of the wives and children of the king.

In the three courtyards are the remains of a small temple, the chapels for the celebration of the *Heb-Sed* jubilee festival, and two buildings known as the South House and the North House. The *serdab* adjoining the north side of the pyramid is interesting. It is a small sealed chamber containing a statue of Djoser, pierced at the level of the eyes to allow him to maintain a vigil over the world (the sculpture is a copy of the original now conserved in the Museum of Cairo). The remains of the funerary temple are also located on the north side of the pyramid.

The southern side of the Djoser wall contained the enigmatic South Tomb, equipped with a funerary temple (external) and an important hypostyle section at the bottom of a shaft. Beyond the wall, to the south, stands the small, Fifth Dynasty pyramid of Unas. While the exterior of this monument is badly damaged, the interior is of great interest. The antechamber and the burial chamber feature well preserved hieroglyphic engravings of passages from the earlier Pyramid Texts. To the south of the enclosure wall of the pyramid of Unis is the tomb of Maya, the treasurer to Tutankhamun. Discovered in 1986, the tomb is made of three rooms decorated with hieroglyphs and figured scenes. The sarcophagus and the funerary furnishings can be seen in the Museum of Cairo. Another vast funerary complex is the one attributed to the Sekhemkhet, the successor to Djoser, who ruled for seven years. The enclosure housed a step pyramid. The entrance shaft led to a subterranean area with 132 chambers where an empty alabaster sarcophagus was found.

In the northeast of the site, immediately adjacent to the enclosing wall, are located the ruins of the pyramid of Userkaf (2465-2458 B.C.), the founder of the Fifth Dynasty, and a short distance to the east, the remains of the pyramid of Tety (2323-2291 B.C.), founder of the Sixth Dynasty.

THE MASTABAS

The mastabas are tombs of a parallelepiped shape, sized according to the importance of their owners. The external structure is composed of one or more chapels giving access to the hypostyle chambers by way of a staircase or a shaft. There are numerous well preserved examples at Saqqara.

The decoration of the mastabas represents the highest expression of the figurative art of the Old Kingdom. Of particular interest is the tomb of Mereruka and his wife Sesheshet. With its 32 rooms, this is the largest and most complex of the Old Kingdom mastabas. Decorations with everyday subject matter such as hunting and fishing scenes, domestic and wild animals, farmers, laborers, and craftsmen at work, and family portraits have provided Egyptologists with insights into the daily lives of the ancient Egyptians.

Other significant mastabas in the area are those of Kagemni and, in particular, Ty. The fascinating relief decorations in the latter are among the most beautiful from the Old Kingdom.

102-103
*Ten multicolored statues
sculpted in the living rock
are aligned inside the tomb
of Irukaptah.*

103 bottom left
*A view of one of the rooms
inside the mastaba of
Kagemni at Saqqara.*

103 bottom right
*Bas-relief depicting a
funerary procession, located
in one of the private tombs
at Saqqara.*

104-105
Bearers on the south wall of the offering room in the mastaba of Ti.

106-107
Men harvesting while a flock of goats is led into a field; from the mastaba of Mehu.

Dahshur and surrounding area

This is the southernmost site of the great Cairo archaeological area and is located a few miles south of Saqqara, the royal necropolis of the Old and Middle Kingdoms. Dahshur features five pyramids, all of which are still visible today. Two of these are of great interest and are both attributed to the pharaoh Snefru, the founder of the Fourth Dynasty (2575-2551 B.C.). Of the pair, the southern one is known as the "Bent Pyramid" due to the double inclination of its faces, while the second, known as the "Red Pyramid" features the same inclination as the upper section of the Bent Pyramid, but a less steep slope than that of the Great Pyramid at Giza. Both pyramids are over 295 feet high, are built in stone, and have an internal burial chamber with a very high ceiling composed of projecting slabs of stone. No sarcophaghi or inscriptions were found inside the Bent Pyramid. However, the excavation brought to light the Lower Temple composed of a courtyard with a colonnade, chambers, and chapels with bas-reliefs. The Red Pyramid, so-named after the color of the stone used, has a broader base and is slightly taller than the bent pyramid. The other three pyramids at Dahshur belong to the pharaohs of the Middle Kingdom, Amenemhat II, Senusret III, and Amenemhat III of the Twelfth Dynasty.

ABU-SIR AND ZAWIYET-AL-ARYAN

While not a habitual stop on the traditional tourist routes, these two sites feature elements of great archaeological interest.

Abu-Sir is the necropolis of the Fifth Dynasty,

108 top
Aerial view of the pyramids of Neferirkara (bottom) and Niuserra (top) at Abusir.

108 center top
The elegant profile of the Red Pyramid at Dahshur.

108 center bottom
Another view of the Abu-sir complex; on the left note the unfinished pyramid of Neferefra.

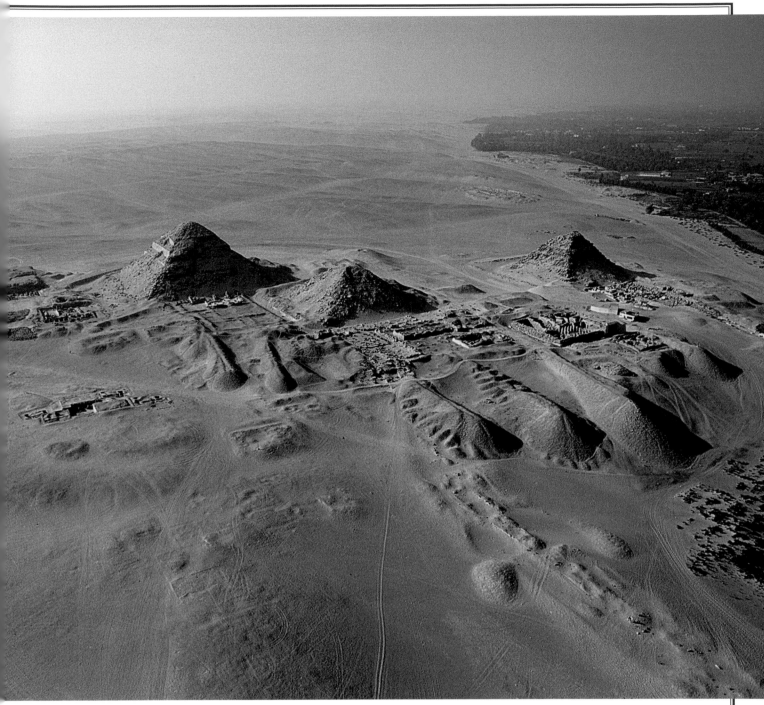

the area of the Solar Temples, and lots of pyramids. Most of these are ruined, but the constructions of the pharaohs Sahura, Neferirkara, and Nyuserra give precise information about the characteristics of the funerary monuments of the Fifth Dynasty (2465-2323 B.C.). The pharaohs of this dynasty declared themselves to be descendants of the sun god Ra and the temples represented the point of conjunction between the sovereign and his divine origins. The obelisks (known as *tekhen* to the ancient Egyptians) located inside the sanctuary above a truncated pyramid date from this period.

The obelisk was a symbolic representation of the god Ra of Heliopolis and could, like the pyramids, be interpreted as the petrification of the sun's rays or the sacred primordial stone from

which the sun rose. The monuments found at Abu-Sir are less impressive than those of Giza, but feature a greater stylistic elegance. The austere rectangular pilasters give way to columns representing bundles of reeds with capitals sculpted in the form of date palm leaves. The walls are decorated with bas-reliefs although, unfortunately, most of these were destroyed by vandalism during the past centuries.

Temples and tombs, at Abu-Sir, are precisely aligned along the course of the Nile, as at Giza. The lower temples were probably lapped by the waters of the river. The excavations of an unbuilt pyramid and the ruins of a second pyramid from the Third Dynasty can be found in the Zawiyet-al-Aryan area.

108 bottom
The unmistakable shape of the Bent Pyramid at Dahshur.

108-109
Another fine aerial view of the Abusir complex, with the three pyramids surrounded by the vast necropolis.

The Oases

The word "oasis," used by the Egyptians and then Herodotus to describe the areas of vegetation in the Libyan Desert to the west of the Nile, meant "cauldron." The oases are, in effect, depressions in the ground that are almost impermeable and therefore rich in wells and springs that since ancient times have permitted the practice of agriculture, and in particular viticulture. The ancient text of Edfu, dating from the Ptolemaic Period, mentioned seven oases, including those of Kharga, Dakhla, Farafra, Bahariya, Siwa, and Faiyum.

These oases were inhabited in prehistoric times and here the established tribes were more advanced than those of the Nile valley. From the earliest dynasties, the pharaohs made sure they occupied many of these areas given their strategic importance and the value of their inhabitants as desert guides.

FAIYUM

The oasis of Al Faiyum is a vast cultivated area to the south-west of Cairo. It is principally irrigated by the Bahr Yussuf (the River of Joseph), a canal linking the oasis to the river and flowing into Birket Qarun (known to the ancients as the Moeris). Traditionally dedicated to the crocodile divinity Sobek, the name of the oasis was derived from the Coptic word *Phiom*, meaning lake or sea, which itself derived from the Egyptian word of the same meaning *Pa iam*. The absence of a flow of water draining the area meant that vast swamps were created arund the oasis with luxuriant vegetation and a richly varied fauna, conditions that made Faiyum a favorite hunting area of the pharaohs. A number of Twelfth Dynasty sovereigns undertook large-scale reclamation projects, increasing the tillable land by means of a complex network of canals and locks that attracted a great number of colonists to the area.

Al Faiyum enjoyed a period of great expansion during the Middle Kingdom and, thanks to the ingenious hydraulic systems mentioned by Strabo and Herodotus, Birket Qarun was raised six feet above sea level. The Macedonian, Greek, and Hebrew colonists built new cities such as Crocodilopolis, Karanis, and Dionysus, while Al Faiyum became the center of Hellenistic culture in Egypt. Numerous Greek and Egyptian papyruses came from these cities, but the most unusual archaeological finds are the numerous portraits of ordinary people executed in encaustic on wood for funerary purposes. The oasis prospered for centuries until the lake shrank to its present size following the administrative decadence that characterized the whole of Egypt in the third century A.D.

Karanis features the ruins of the temple of Nero dedicated to the crocodile deities, Pnepheros and Petosukos. A great number of mummified examples of these reptiles have also been discovered, probably dedicated to Sobek.

110 top
One of the lion-headed sphinxes that adorned the dromos of the temple of Medinet Madi in Faiyum.

110 center top
The ruins of the north temple of Karanis, in Faiyum.

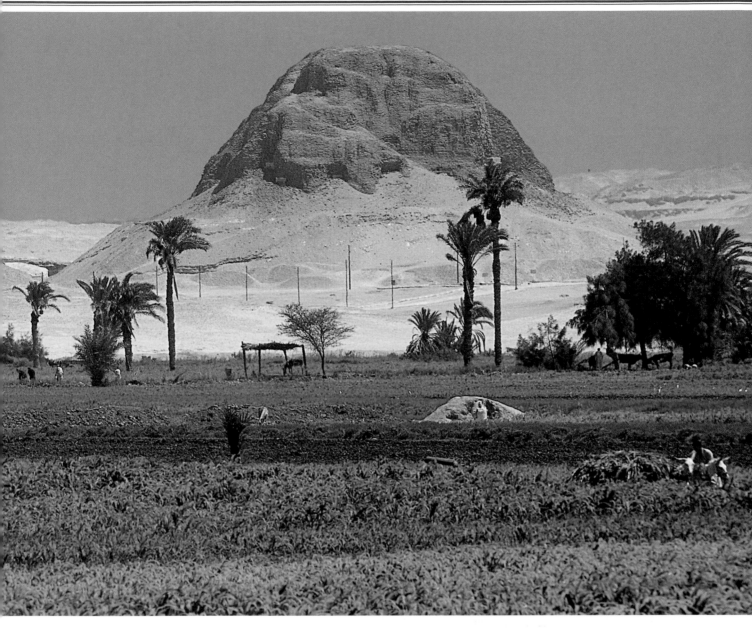

Around 6 miles to the south-west stand the ruins of Dimet, the ancient Soknopaiu Nesos, or Island of Sobek. On the southern side is the 9,312-foot long processional avenue running alongside the temple which still contains relief sculptures showing Ptolemy II praying to the god Amun.

Close to the village of Biahmu stood two imposing colossal statues of Amenemhat III which were seen by Herodotus during his journey through Egypt and also mentioned by a traveler in 1700. Today, all that remain here are the bases and a few fragments of the statues currently displayed in the Ashmolean at Oxford. Medinet Al Faiyum instead features the obelisk of Senusret I (Twelfth Dynasty), erected at the center of a cross-roads.

The village of Al Maqta boasts the ruins of the brick pyramid of Hawara, built by Amenemhat III and, further to the south, the few remains of his huge funerary temple with the 12 courtyards which inspired Greek travelers to call it "Labyrinth."

110 center bottom
The temple of Amenemhat III at Medinet Madi.

110 bottom right
A view of the Oasis of Faiyum.

110-111
The pyramid of al-Lahun, in Faiyum.

111 bottom left
The temple of Qasr Qarun in Faiyum.

111 bottom center
Interior of the temple of Qasr Qarun.

111 bottom right
Interior of the temple of Medinet Masi in Faiyum.

112
The temple of Ibis in the Kharga Oasis.

113 top left
One of the great gateways in front of the temple of Ibis.

113 center top
The ruins of Qasr Dush, a temple dedicated to Serapis, to the south of Kharga.

113 center bottom
The Dakhla Oasis: the temple of Deir al-Hagiar.

113 top right
Multicolored bas-relief inside the temple of Deir al-Hagiar.

113 right center top
The Siwa Oasis, with one of the characteristic rocky outcrops.

113 right center bottom
The celebrated Temple of the Oracle in the Siwa Oasis.

113 bottom right
The ruins of the temple of Amun, in the Siwa Oasis.

KHARGA

The oases of Kharga and Dakhla, located to the west of Thebes and constantly under Egyptian control, boast ancient monuments still today immersed in unspoiled surroundings. Just to the north of Kharga, known as Al-Khargia in Arabic, rise the ruins of the ancient city of Hibis, with its temple of Amun dedicated to the god by Darius I, restored and extended by Nectanebo II and then further enlarged during the Graeco-Roman Period.

The temple features a classic layout with pylons, a courtyard, and a hypostyle hall. There is an interesting depiction of the god Seth in the act of transfixing the serpent Apopis with a spear. Seth, a deity initially seen as a benevolent protector of the oases, had a far darker image in the Nile valley. It should be noted that the deity's slaying of the serpent with a spear was a motif taken up in Christian iconography with St. George and the dragon. Around a half mile to the north of the temple, are the ruins of the Christian necropolis of Al-Baqawat. A number of the chapels have pictorial decorations with biblical themes and symbolic figures, some of which are still well preserved.

DAKHLA

This oasis, Al-Dakhila in Arabic, is renowned for its great natural beauty and proverbial tranquility. This is the largest of the oases in the Western Desert and is located around 217 miles from the Nile. It was discovered by Bernardino Drovetti of Piedmont in 1819.

There are few ruins in the area: the lythic tomb of Kitines and the remains of the temple of Mut, built during the Eighteenth and Nineteenth Dynasties and subsequently restored by Rameses IX. The mastabas of governors from the Old Kingdom have recently been discovered *in situ*, confirming the interest the vast oasis held for the ancient Egyptians of the Nile Valley.

FARAFRA

Farafra, or Al-Farafira, was known to the ancient Egyptians as "Taith," the "Land of the Cow." Archaeological excavations recently undertaken have identified the remains of houses from Predynastic periods. There is, instead, no trace of the presence of the pharaohs, in spite of the oasis being mentioned in documents from the Fifth Dynasty onwards. Close to Qasr Farafra, the interesting town surrounded by walls, stands an ancient necropolis with rock tombs.

SIWA

It is said that immediately after founding Alexandria, Alexander the Great undertook a long and gruelling journey to the oasis of Siwa in order to consult the oracle of Jupiter-Amemnon.

The oasis of Siwa only came under Egyptian control during the Ptolemaic Period due to its remoteness (342 miles from Cairo) and the hostility of the local people. In ancient times, the Libyans and the inhabitants of the oases consecrated it to a native deity called Amemnon by the Egyptians and Greeks. The remains of the temples of Aghurmi and Umm al-Beda, probably dating from the Saitic period, are the only ruins left.

114 top
Bas-relief in a tomb at Beni Hasan.

114 center top
The gilded plaster mask of one of the mummies discovered in the Bahariya Oasis.

BAHARIYA OR (WAHAT AL-) BAHRIYYA

Wahat al-Bahriyya means "Oasis of the Sea" or "Northern Oasis" and is situated in a deep depression to the west of Al Faiyum. The oasis still houses the remains of a Twenty-sixth Dynasty temple, inscriptions in the chapel of the pharaoh Apries revealing that the complex was dedicated to Amun-Ra, "Lord of the great hill," and to the god Khonsu who, along with his parents Amun and Mut, was part of the triad of Thebes.

The rock tombs of the nobles situated behind the slope of the village are also interesting, the oldest being that of the governor Amenothep from the Eighteenth Dynasty. Although in poor condition, it still retains some of the original colors.

The burial complex of the ibises at Qarat al-Fararji has to date given up a number of mummified corpses of these birds, as well as amulets. The oasis has aroused international interest both for the remains of its Roman monuments and the very recent discovery of the so-called "necropolis of the golden mummies" by Zahi Hawass's Egyptian team. Over 105 mummies from the Graeco-Roman epoch have been recovered, but it is estimated that there are over 10,000 in total. This necropolis is located close to the temple of Alexander the Great and was discovered by chance in 1996 when a watchman returning home from work with his donkey noticed that the animal's hoof had sunk into the ground. Immediate excavations brought to light a number of mummies.

BENI HASAN

Beni Hasan is located halfway between the ancient royal cities of Memphis and Thebes, in an area of palm groves and green fields close to the Nile. An ancient Middle Kingdom necropolis, its 39 tombs are almost all situated along the side of the hill. Only a few are open to the public, but they are all of interest and contain scenes of agriculture, hunting, and sport.

Tomb No. 17, which still has two of its original six columns, features scenes of wrestling,

114 center bottom
A view of the tomb of Bannantiu, discovered in the Bahariya Oasis.

114

114 bottom
Interior of one of the tombs at Beni Hasan.

114-115
The Egyptian archaeologist Zahi Hawass cleaning sand from some mummies from the Bahariya Oasis.

115 bottom
Another detail of a tomb at Beni Hasan.

hunting, and dance in sequential scenes of movement of such accuracy as to create the impression of cinematic frames. The tomb was constructed at the behest of the high priest Kethi, who is portrayed wearing the typical sacerdotal leopard-skin robes. Tomb No. 15, which belonged to governor of the *nome*, Baket, the father of Kethi, is similar, while Tomb No.3 belonging to Khnumhotep, another local *nomarch* and governor, is famous for its drawings depicting hunting and fishing scenes. The columns of these hypogea are in the style defined by Champollion as "Proto-Doric." The expedition led by the Frenchman and the Tuscan Ippolito Rossellini between 1828 and 1829 spent much time here and made accurate drawings of the interiors.

In 1891, the Egypt Exploration society despatched the young archaeologist Percy Newbarry to work here with a talented young draftsman, Howard Carter.

Tell al-Amarna

Around 40 miles from the city of Al Minya in central Egypt stand the ruins of Akhenaten, capital of the Amarnian religious revolution named after the present-day city of Tell al-Amarna. The city was founded by the Eighteenth Dynasty pharaoh, Amenhotep IV, better known by the new name he chose for himself, Akhenaten. Close to the present day village of Al-Till, the confines of this ephemeral capital are delineated within an area enclosed by rocky walls

extending for almost 2 miles along the banks of the Nile. The city was founded on virgin soil and inhabited for no more than thirty years. Amenhotep IV had the courage to make a definitive stand against the power of the Theban sacerdotal class. If it is true that this king, apparently a lover of art and nature, rejected the idea of war *a priori*, it is perhaps plausible that the instrument of religion appeared to him to be more efficient and painless. The proclamation of a single god, Aten, the solar disc, and the obscuring of all the Theban deities, including Amun, perhaps created a pressing need for a new center from which to officiate the cult of the sun without having to accept pre-existing architectural compromises. This was probably the reason why the pharaoh abandoned Thebes in around the fifth year of his reign and hurriedly built this new capital as careful study of the ruins has revealed. The city was designed in accordance with the worship of a sun god who, each dawn in a daily cyclical ritual, illuminated the rich colors of the buildings and temples. After its destruction by the Theban avengers, Akhenaten was abandoned and fell into oblivion for centuries.

Towards the end of the 19th century, F. Petrie began a series of systematic excavations with the help of a young artist, Howard Carter, destined to achive immense fame with the discovery of the tomb of Tutankhamun. Subsequently, the site was also studied and excavated by German and British teams. Clear references to the city's foundation were discovered on one of the stelae marking its confines. The hieroglyphs reveal that "on the thirteenth day of the eighth month of the sixth year [of the king's reign] the king, riding in a golden carriage, left the rich tent where he had spent the night and traveled to mark the confines of the city of Akhenaten. After making an offering to the divinity he moved south to a point where the sun's rays indicated to him the southern confines of the city. The sovereign prayed for his royal wife and his children and then swore never to pass these confines."

The temple of Aten was deliberately destroyed following the death of the pharaoh and its stones were reused by Rameses II for his temple at Hermopolis Magna. The foundations reveal the shape of the building, a rectangle 2,625 by 902 feet. The first pylon was followed by a hypostyle hall, covered on either side with the central nave left open. Then came various courtyards separated by porticoes, with some altars raised on platforms of unfired brick and located along the temple axis in rows of four. The last room was devoted to the liturgical ceremonies concerning the encounter with the deity. Nearby are the surviving foundations of storerooms that served the religious complex.

The palace featured the royal couple's private courtyards and apartments where archaeologists found the image of Akhenaten and Nefertiti sitting facing each other on a large cushion, surrounded by their six daughters. The image is currently conserved in the Ashmolean at Oxford. The entire

residence was decorated with scenes of nature and everyday life, these last displaying a decisive break with the rigid traditional models. It appears that the sovereigns also chose to have themselves portrayed realistically and we can thus be certain of the remarkable beauty of Nefertiti and the partial physical deformation of her consort. Clay tablets were brought to light in the nearby palace archive that documented, in cuneiform characters, the diplomatic correspondence between the pharaohs Amenhotep III, Akhenaten, and Tutankhamun and the Asiatic kings and Syrian vassal states. The most sensational find was made in the proximity of the court buildings: the workshop of the craftsman Thutmosis, containing a number of sculpted busts. One of these, probably belonging to Nephertitis, is colored and in perfect condition and is on display in the Egyptian Museum in Berlin.

The city's necropolis is to be found in the hills to the east. The tomb paintings, in contrast with those of Thebes, do not contain scenes of the underworld; the so-called process of psychostasia practiced before Osiris is completely absent here. The paintings instead show vivid representations of terrestrial life. Many of the tombs were unfinished with few showing signs of actually having been used for a burial. It appears that the Amarnian counter-revolution interrupted the eternal rest the necropolis was designed to guarantee the defunct nobles of the city of the sun.

Akhenaten's mummy has long been searched for, both here and at Thebes, but to date the research has proved fruitless, despite the fact that the royal tomb was found in these hills at Darb al-Malik.

118-119
The imposing remains of the temple of Rameses II.

118 bottom left
Bas-reliefs from the temple of Rameses II.

118 bottom right
Rameses II in front of the offerings to the gods.

Abydos

Situated on the west bank of the Nile, about 90 miles north of Luxor, Abydos was originally the principal necropolis of the nearby city of This, or Thinis, the first capital of a united Egypt. The site was, in fact, chosen as a necropolis by the kings of the first dynasties (early in the third millennium B.C.). The city also became a pilgrimage destination for those seeking at least a symbolic burial in the form of a stela set as close as possible to the tomb of the god Osiris, of whose cult Abydos was the center. Legend has it that the deity's head was buried here after his brother Seth had killed and dismembered him. Around 350 tombs, some of royal origin, have been brought to light in the area of the Thinite necropolis. These tombs range from the most modest composed of a trench in the ground, to more elaborate constructions which housed high ranking figures.

Tombs of sacred animals have also been discovered at Abydos, necropolises for jackals, the embodiment of the god Anubis, ibises, the incarnation of the god Thot, and falcons symbolizing the god Horus.

THE TEMPLE OF SETY I

The construction of the Temple of Abydos dedicated to Osiris, was begun by Sety I and completed by his son Rameses II with the addition of a pylon and two courtyards now ruined.

The facade we see today is not the true temple facade, but rather a portico with twelve columns that acted as the backdrop to the second great courtyard. The covered temple and the first hypostyle hall were reached via a ramp. The layout of the building was organized on the basis of the sacred numbers two and seven. There are, in fact, two pylons, two courtyards, and two hypostyle halls, seven doors opening onto the internal section and seven bays that traverse the two hypostyle halls and lead to the seven chapels constituting the heart of the temple.

The lateral walls of the first hypostyle hall, with its two transverse rows of twelve columns, and the second with three rows of twelve columns, delineate the passages to the seven shrines dedicated to Sety I, Osiris, Isis, Horus, Amun, Mut, and Khonsu. The first hall measuring 171 x 36 feet is divided into seven chapels dedicated to seven different deities. The second hall, the same size as the first, features columns with papyrus capitals and is characterized by a converging floor and ceiling. Of the seven chapels, the one dedicated to Osiris has significant differences compared with the other six which each house a stela on the back wall. In the Osiris chapel instead, a passage opens from the back wall and leads to another temple dedicated to Osiris, Isis, and Horus and composed of a principal hall supported by ten columns leading to three chapels. An unusual feature of this secondary temple of Osiris is the presence in the northwest corner of a small room with two columns lacking any form of aperture and therefore inaccessible, as if to symbolize the fact that the secret of the mysteries of Abydos will remain inviolate.

The left-hand part of the temple opens onto a hall with three columns and two chapels consecrated to the gods Nefertim and Ptah Sokaris respectively. Both of these gods were funerary deities associated with the rituals of resurrection.

119 top
Bas-relief depicting Rameses II embraced by the goddess Isis.

119 bottom
The facade of the temple of Sety I, punctuated by 12 pilasters.

A long corridor leading to the South Halls features a ceiling with stars and royal cartouches, the symbolism of which is explicit: the spirit of the dead king rises to heaven to join the light and become a star. From the corridor one reaches the six southern halls: the first was used as a storeroom for the boats used during processions, while the remaining five were used as storerooms for sacred objects. Leading off this corridor is a flight of steps that once gave access to the roof and which today leads to the cenotaph.

THE CENOTAPH OF SETY I (OSIREION)

The term cenotaph indicates a particular type of false tomb which does not contain a body, being symbolically dedicated to the deceased's spirit alone. The cenotaph of Sety I at Abydos, to be considered as the spiritual tomb of Osiris, dates back to before the Nineteenth Dynasty and was discovered in 1903 beneath a vast mass of rubble. Sety I, whose own tomb is located in the Valley of the Kings, transformed this "virtual tomb" into the colossal work we see today. Today the cenotaph is reached by way of the Temple of Sety I, but the original entrance was situated to the north-west of the building and was composed of shafts dug in the desert. This was, in fact, a type of entrance that only the spirit of the deceased was able to penetrate in order to reach the crypt. The nucleus is composed of a hall with ten pilasters symbolizing the island at the center of the world that emerged from the waters at the creation of the universe. During the Nile floods, the cenotaph symbolized an island surrounded by water. The Osireion features two niches, one square and one rectangular, which in all probability contained the sarcophagus and canopic vases of the god Osiris.

120-121
The great hypostyle hall of the temple of Sety I, supported by three rows of 36 columns each.

120 bottom right
A view of the upper nave of the second hypostyle hall in the temple of Sety I.

120 bottom left
Bas-relief inside the naos dedicated to Horus, with the god handing over the sceptre of power to the pharaoh.

121 right
A view of the first hypostyle hall, in which the papyrus columns supporting the ceiling can be seen clearly.

Behind the hall with the pilasters is the last hall of the temple, the true inner sanctum, an elongated rectangle in shape with a pitched roof. The hall is decorated with astrological and astronomical inscriptions and images.

THE TEMPLE OF RAMESES II

The temple of Ramsees II is a small complex around 980 feet northwest of the temple of Sety I, but very little has survived to the present day.

Construction work probably began during the era of Sety I, the resulting monument being one of the principal temples dedicated to Rameses II. The original structure was composed of two pylons and two courtyards, an entrance hall with a single portico, two hypostyle halls, and a shrine with three chapels. The first pylon and the first courtyard have been lost and visitors therefore enter the complex through the second pylon which is itself ruined. The second courtyard was distinguished by the presence of 26 Osirian columns. Numerous relief sculptures show scenes of ritual sacrifices and offerings to the gods. The upper part of the temple has collapsed, thus depriving us of the scenes which once decorated the hypostyle halls and the shrine.

Dendera

The city of Dendera is located around 40 miles north of Luxor on the site of the ancient Junet, capital of the sixth *nome* of Upper Egypt. All that remains today is a Ptolemaic Period temple dedicated to the goddess Hathor and dating from the first century B.C.

The goddess Hathor, symbolically represented by a woman with the ears of a cow, was venerated here as the divinity of the cosmos in which life takes form. Hathor (whose name means Temple of Horus) in fact represents the maternal womb in which Horus — life itself —

was conceived. Hathor is also known as the goddess of love, the source of joy for living creatures. It is no coincidence that one of her most frequent symbols is a *sistrum*, a musical instrument whose vibrations dispersed negative influences and attracted positive ones. The Temple of Dendera is known as the Sistrum Temple as it was conceived as an enormous musical instrument in which the harmonies of the cosmos were brought together.

The building was originally surrounded by triple curtain walls built of brick, but only the Hathor wall around the heart of the sacred complex survives today. Within the walls stood a sacred lake — upon which scenes from the mysteries of Osiris were represented, with the lake becoming the primordial ocean, source of life — and two *mammisi* (temples of birth).

The facade of the temple features six columns representing the goddess' musical instruments, surmounted by the head of Hathor. For each sistrum there are four heads facing towards the four cardinal points.

The entrance to the covered temple leads into a hypostyle hall, where two groups of nine columns stand on either side of the central axis. The ceiling is painted with cosmic and astrological scenes, while heaven is represented by the goddess Nut, who each evening swallowed the sun in order to regenerate it during the night and restore it to the world the following morning.

There follows the hall of apparitions with the ceiling supported by six columns and with three rooms on either side. On the left is the workshop and on the right is the treasury where the alchemists produced unguents, oils, and precious materials. There follow the calendar and Nile rooms, which had the function of measuring the rhythm of the seasons to which

122 top
The king is making offerings to Hathor in a relief of the Roman mammisi, at Dendera.

122 center
The remains of two mammisis and a Christian church, in front of the temple.

122 bottom
A side view of the Roman-period mammisi.

122-123
The 138-foot wide temple
facade.

123 bottom left
The intercolumns of the
mammisi, *covered with reliefs.*

123 bottom right
The rear facade of the temple
of Hathor.

124
The ceiling of the great hypostyle hall, with the astronomical decorations.

125 right center top
A multicolor relief showing the solar disc of Amun-Ra that illuminates the goddess Hathor.

125 left
Magnificent examples of Hathoric capitals.

125 right center bottom
The entrance of the Hathoric chapel.

125 top right
A series of bas-reliefs inside the mammisi.

125 bottom right
The corridor running around the perimeter of the naos.

the prosperity of the country was closely bound. The central room or Ennead Hall, was the place in which a hymn was recited to reawaken the divinity.

Below the temple are twelve crypts set on three levels and representing the underworld. The small rooms were used to conserve the objects required for the cult of the goddess and were considered to be the places in which the divine forces regenerated themselves in silence.

The top of the temple is in part occupied by the terrace destined for the annual celebration of the union with the solar disc, when the statue of the goddess was directly exposed to the sunlight so that it could be "charged" with positive energy. To the north of the terrace, a chapel dedicated to Osiris — a place symbolically associated with resurrection — is particularly interesting because it features a copy of the celebrated circular zodiac, the only such example realized in Egypt. The original is now conserved in Paris. In 1820, Sebastien Saulnier, a member of the French parliament, instructed the builder Jean Baptiste Lelorrain to remove the zodiac. Lelorrain eventually succeeded after a four-week struggle. The zodiac reached Paris in the January of 1822 and

was acquired by the king for the royal library. It was finally transferred to the Louvre in 1919. The sandstone bas-relief measures 8.4 x 8.3 feet, with the central disc having a diameter of 5.1 feet. The circle containing the astronomical representation is supported by four pairs of falcon-headed deities and the four divinities of the cardinal points.

A sacred building dedicated to the birth of Isis, the great sovereign spirit of the sacred sites of Egypt and the bringer of life, was erected behind the great temple of Hathor.

Two unusual buildings are to be found at Dendera: the first, to the right of the great courtyard, is the sanatorium where the sick came for thermal treatment (it was not a public building as it was located within the temple walls), and the second is the *mammisi* (the "House of Birth"), a place consecrated to the celebration of the birth of a son conceived by the gods.

The significance of the *mammisi* (a building typical of the Egyptian temples of the Graeco-Roman Period) is illustrated by the relief sculptures that decorate it: a sacred marriage and the birth of a divine son, with specific references to the youth of the creator gods.

Luxor

Arriving at Luxor in the evening, with the sun setting behind the mountains that conceal the desert, one cannot help being entranced by the gently blending colors that rapidly transform the landscape.

The Nile flows slowly and lights in the first houses among the palms on the west bank begin to be lit. If we then look up at the almost always clear sky, we see a particularly bright star descend slowly in the midnight blue before disappearing, much later, behind the western mountains. This star was known to the ancient Egyptians as Sothis and was associated with Isis.

This spectacle has been repeated for millennia, long before Theses, Luxor, and Karnak came into existence. Thebes, the magnificent and wealthy capital of the glorious dynasties and princes who liberated Egypt from the invaders, white Thebes of the hundred doors celebrated by the Greeks, the sacred city of Amun, Mut and Khonsu, is no more.

Today, all that remains of ancient Thebes are the temples of Karnak and Luxor, together with a few other ruins which we can still admire but which we are obliged to recognize as mere fragments of past splendors.

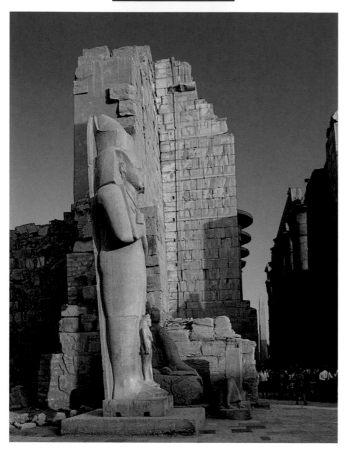

THE TEMPLE OF KARNAK

The stones of the vast archaeological area of Karnak recount well over 13 centuries of history. The buildings here range from the early foundations of the temple erected in the Middle Kingdom to the first pylon probably constructed during the late Thirtieth Dynasty. The god of war, Montu, associated with Thebes during the Old Kingdom, was the first to suffer from the overwhelming rise of the cult of Amun during the Middle Kingdom, as testified to by the construction of temples facing west. With the expulsion of the Hyksos from the country and beginning of the Eighteenth Dynasty, "Ipet Isut" or the "Elected Place," became the most important sanctuary in Egypt from spiritual, political, and economic points of view.

Amun was considered to be the god that conquered the enemies of Egypt and the various pharaohs such as Amenhotep and Thutmosis I built chapels around pre-existing monuments, identifying themselves in the form of this divinity.

Queen Hatshepsut added two obelisks in front of the ones installed by her father. Thutmosis III enriched Karnak with the building of the southern *propylaeum* that led, via the avenue of Sphinxes, to the temple of the mother goddess, Mut. During the centuries between the pharaoh's Asian conquests and the reign of Amenhotep III, art and architecture saw the establishment of the so-called imperial style, seen at Karnak in the third pylon built by Amenhotep III.

Work began on the great hypostyle hall, subsequently extended by Sety I and his son Rameses II. Foreign influences favored by the

128 top
The capitals of the central nave have a diameter of 49 feet at the summit.

128 bottom
The statue of Rameses II and, in the background, the columns of the hypostyle hall.

128-129
A 69-foot high column stands in the great courtyard, the sole surviving element of a kiosk built at the behest of the Ethiopian king Taharqa around 680 B.C.

LEGEND

A Access *dromos*
B Enclosure wall of Precinct of Amun
C Temple of Rameses III
D Great hypostyle hall
E Obelisks
F Wadjit (small hypostyle hall)
G Courtyard of the Middle Kingdom
H Akhmenu
I Temple of Ptah
J Sacred Lake
K Temple of Opet
L Temple of Khonsu
M 7th pylon
N 8th pylon
O 9th pylon
P 10th pylon
Q 1st pylon (of Nectanebo I)
R 2nd pylon
S 3rd pylon
T 4th pylon

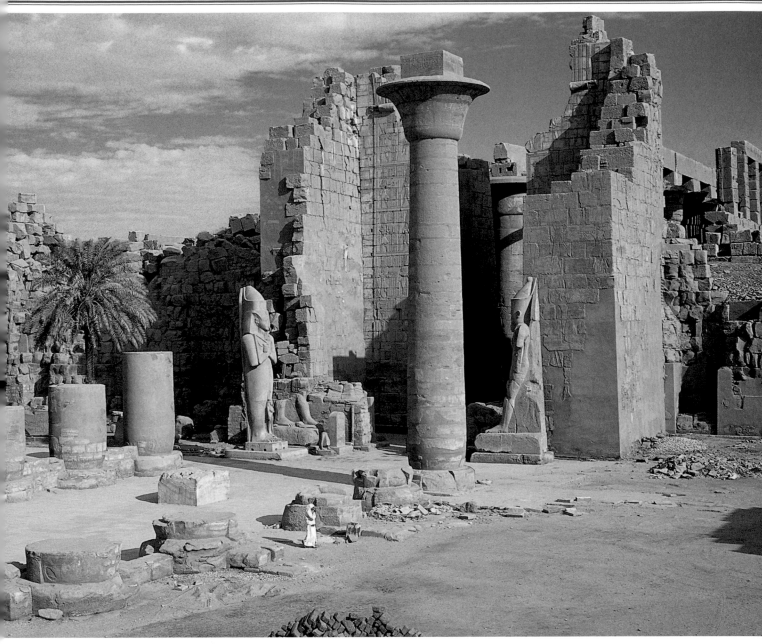

empire brought new wealth to the country and Amun, who had accompanied and lent strength to the pharaoh's military campaigns, saw the temple of Karnak, with its sacerdotal castes and the old aristocracy that had supported it, extend its power until it became a center of power in the country. At the height of its glory, the temple possessed around 81,000 slaves with their families, 240,000 head of livestock and 83 ships, and also received tributes of gold, silver, jewels, and precious stones from over 65 cities around the country.

In this period there was an increasingly clear distinction between the interests of the pharaoh and those of the sacerdotal class. The inevitable conflict was to explode over the following years under Amenhotep IV, son of Amenhotep III. During his reign a radical religious upheaval took place that was to torment Egypt for almost a quarter of a century. Initially, the new pharaoh also

129 bottom
A suggestive view of the great hypostyle hall.

130-131
The enormous religious site at Karnak was dedicated to the Theban triad of gods Amun, Mut, and Khonsu.

132-133
This aerial view shows the magnificent architecture of the sacred complex at Karnak.

134-135
Bas-relief inside the naos
in which is depicted the
coronation of Philip
Arrhidaeus (upper register)
and a procession of priests
transporting the sacred
barque (lower register).

134 bottom
One of the thousands of
bas-reliefs decorating the
Temple of Karnak.

undertook building work at Karnak, but soon transferred the center of power to a site in central Egypt where he intended to build the new city of Akhenaten. The sovereign's new name, Akhenaten, the pharaoh who revealed to the country the cult of Atun, was incised for the first time on the stelae on the east side of the new city. The pharaoh changed his "Horus name" (Powerful Bull With Tall Feathers) which was too closely associated with Thebes, to "Powerful Bull Beloved of Atun," and his "Nebty name" (Great Regal One of Karnak) into "Great Regal One of Akhenaten.

The temple at Karnak suffered severely as a result of this decision, as in transferring the seat of power the pharaoh erased centuries of history and religious tradition, expunging at a stroke the strong religious power of the Amun priesthood. The new religion failed to survive Akhenaten's death, however. The reign of Tutankhamun saw the restoration of the ancient traditions, with Thebes once again becoming the capital of the kingdom and the temple of Karnak reacquiring all its old power. The works of Akhenaten were completely demolished, the stones of his temples being used to reconstruct later shrines.

The second pharaoh of the Nineteenth Dynasty defined his era as "the repeated rebirths," in other words, the era of the renaissance. Both he and his son, Rameses II, enriched Karnak with exceptional buildings. The most grandiose and widely admired work was the completion of the enormous central hypostyle hall.

It was the task of the four successive dynasties to construct the first pylon and the large courtyard and thus bring Karnak to its present size. Even though this marked the onset of a long decline, the cult of Amun continued to enjoy undisputed power, with the pharaoh becoming a mere instrument in the hands of this powerful oligarchy.

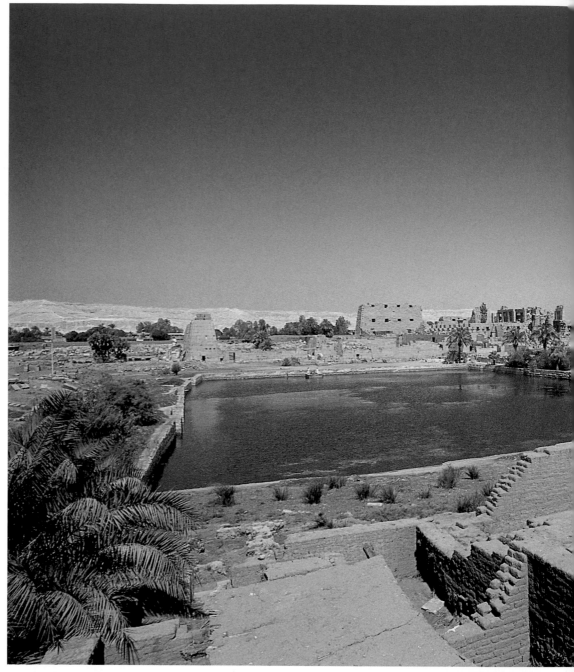

136 top left
One of the great flights of steps that led to the roof of the grandiose temple.

136-137
A panoramic view of the Temple of Karnak, with the sacred lake in the foreground.

136 bottom left
The Osiris pillars in the courtyard of the temple of Rameses III.

136 bottom right
One of the two pillars with the heraldic symbols of Upper and Lower Egypt erected by Thutmosis III.

137 top
The Akh-Menu or feasting hall of Thutmosis III, supported by 20 columns and 32 pilasters.

137 bottom
The god Amun-Ra was the principal divinity worshipped at Karnak.

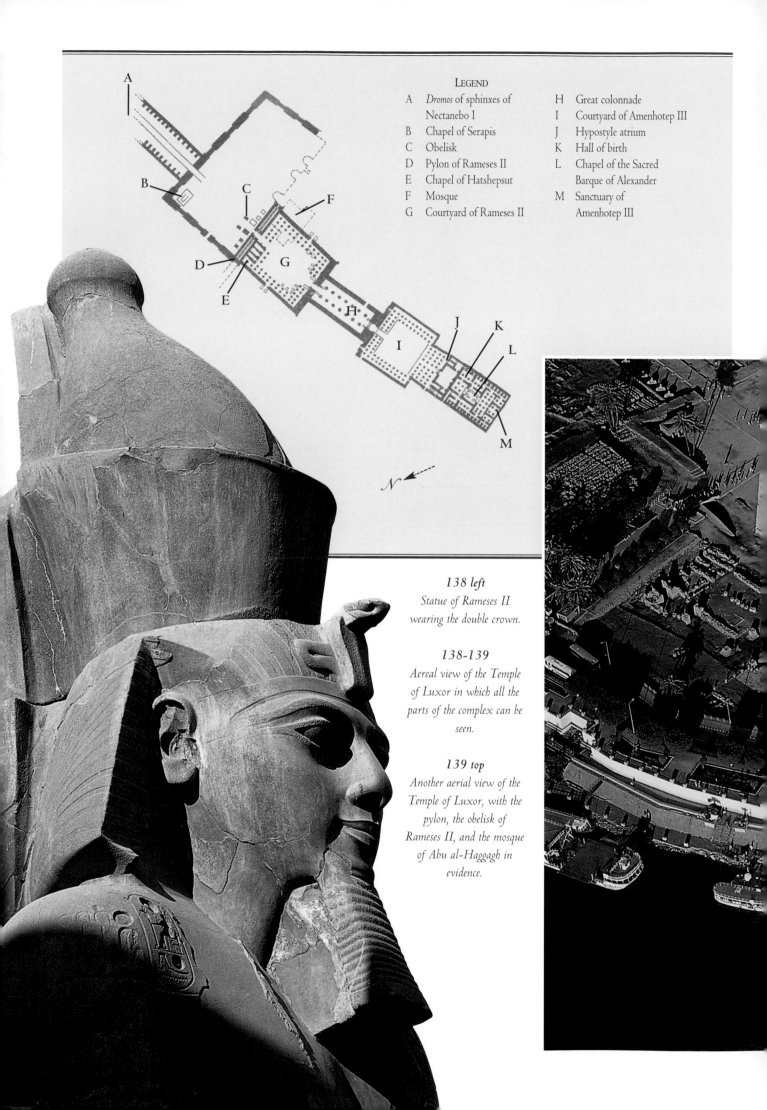

LEGEND

A *Dromos* of sphinxes of Nectanebo I
B Chapel of Serapis
C Obelisk
D Pylon of Rameses II
E Chapel of Hatshepsut
F Mosque
G Courtyard of Rameses II
H Great colonnade
I Courtyard of Amenhotep III
J Hypostyle atrium
K Hall of birth
L Chapel of the Sacred Barque of Alexander
M Sanctuary of Amenhotep III

138 left
Statue of Rameses II wearing the double crown.

138-139
Aereal view of the Temple of Luxor in which all the parts of the complex can be seen.

139 top
Another aerial view of the Temple of Luxor, with the pylon, the obelisk of Rameses II, and the mosque of Abu al-Haggagh in evidence.

THE TEMPLE OF LUXOR

Luxor's present-day name derives from *Al-Uqsor*, the Arab plural of *qasr* meaning castle or construction, and dates from the era of the emperor Diocletian.

The temple of Luxor was constructed almost entirely during the Eighteenth Dynasty by Amenhotep III and Ramsees II and stands on the foundation of an earlier shrine. Under Amenhotep III it became the center of political and religious power for the whole country. It was here that the major religious celebrations were held. During the Nile flood seasons the gold statue of Amun was carried on its sacred barque from Luxor to Karnak. In the mystic atmosphere of the temple, the pharaoh offered gifts and incense to the statue of the god draped in linen. The sacrifices and ceremonies having been completed, the priests carried the deity outside, purifying the road, and then replaced the statue in its barque and returned in procession to Karnak.

Amenhotep was the first pharaoh of the new kingdom to construct monuments of exceptional size designed to convey the new imperialistic ambitions.

Thutmosis III, Hatshepsut, and Tutankhamun contributed to the enlargement of the temple, but it was the great Rameses II who was responsible for substantial additions in the form of two majestic pylons, which he himself defined as "the horizon

from which enters the Sun God," and the vast entrance courtyard. These works of clear military propaganda recount, like the famous "poem of Pentaur," the pharaoh's victory against the Hittites in the battle of Qadesh. Modern Egyptologists nonetheless harbor serious doubts regarding the result of the battle. Of the two 82-foot Ramesside pylons, which up until the first half of the nineteenth century adorned the entrance to the temple, only one remains in its original position; the second was donated to France by Mohammed Ali in 1831 and erected in Place de la Concorde in Paris.

Beyond the pylons and the courtyard stands

141 bottom center
Another view of the human-headed sphinxes which line the access avenue to the temple.

141 bottom
A view of the great colonnade no less than 62 feet high erected at the behest of Amenhotep III.

140-141
The avenue of sphinxes that links the Temple of Luxor (in the background) with that of Karnak.

141 top
One of the numerous sphinxes located in front of the great pylon of the Temple of Luxor.

141 top center
An axial view of the temple from the south-west.

the colonnade of Amenhotep III, featuring papyrus columns around 52 feet high. The true temple begins to unfold with the first antechamber, once protected by a roof supported on eight columns and which later became a chapel for the cult of imperial Rome. Amenhotep III offering gifts and incense to Amun can still be seen in the second antechamber, immediately after which one enters the shrine-chamber of the holy barque of Amun, reconstructed by Alexander the Great and covered with relief sculptures showing the Macedonian emperor making offerings to various deities including the ithyphallic Min.

142 top left
The colonnade of Amenhotep III,
seen from the great
courtyard of Rameses II.

142 center left
A view of the courtyard of
Rameses II, with the north
side of the pylon; on the left
is the sustaining wall of the
mosque of Abu al-Haggagh.

142 bottom left
Detail of the columns
enclosing the courtyard of
Amenhotep III.

142 right
The great pylon of the temple,
fronted by the colossal statues
and obelisk of Rameses II.

143
The base of the obelisk and
one of the two colossal
statues of Rameses II that
stand in front of the pylon.

144-145
Detail of the face of Ramesses
II from one of the granite colossi
that stand in the court in front
of Luxor temple.

THE MUSEUM OF LUXOR

Inaugurated in 1975, the Museum of Luxor conserves a wealth of exceptional relics ranging from jewellery, furniture, and pottery through to stelae and, in particular, boasts statues and busts of great sovereigns such as Senusret III and Thutmosis III (in black basalt, it is one of the most beautiful and best preserved ever found), Amenhotep II, and Amenhotep III. Also worthy of note is an alabaster statue of Sobek, sculpted during the reign of Amenhotep III and successively usurped by Rameses II. Characterized by a human body and a crocodile's head, it is an example of the mastery of Egyptian art during the period of its highest expression.

Mural reliefs representing Akhenaten and Nefertiti in adoration of the solar disc Atun are of notable importance. The sculptures were discovered at Karnak in blocks and skillfully reconstructed here. Visitors may also admire the remarkable statuettes of Tutankhamen in his youth and one of the pharaoh's quivers with a set of arrows discovered in his tomb. An engraving on pink granite tells the story of Queen Hatshepsut's expedition to the land of Punt and the subsequent erection of two obelisks giving thanks to Amun in the temple of Karnak.

In the courtyard in front of the museum are two statues of Amenhotep III and Rameses II.

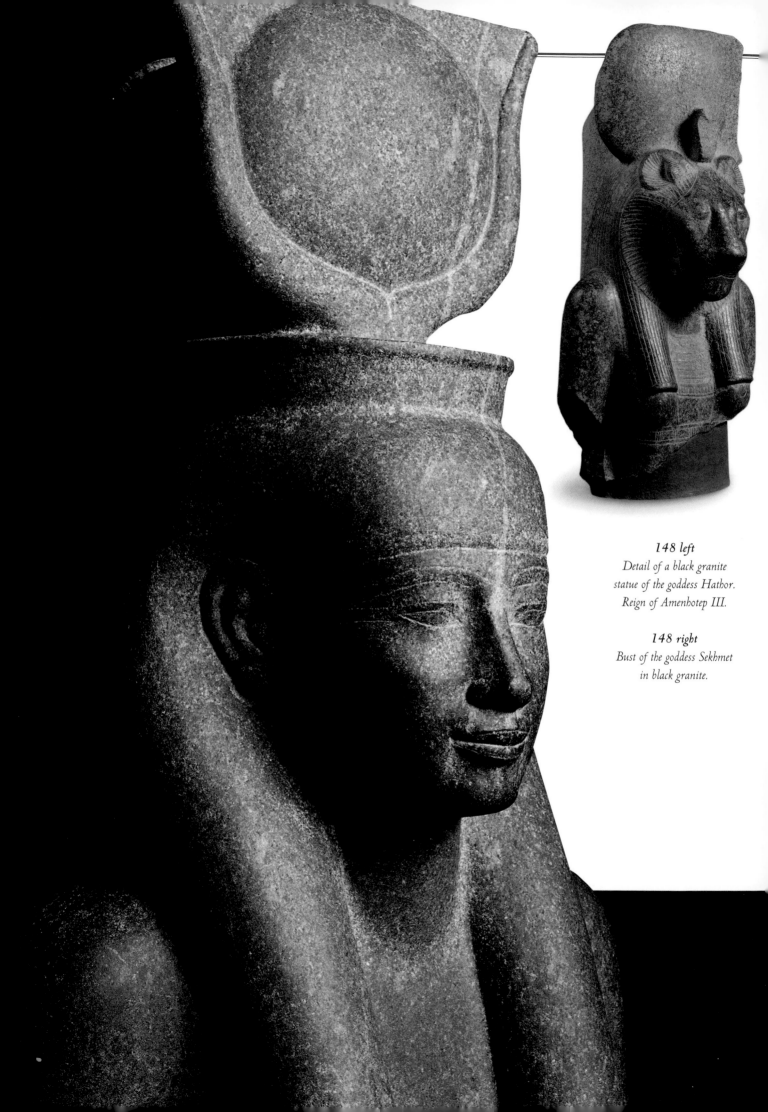

148 left
Detail of a black granite statue of the goddess Hathor. Reign of Amenhotep III.

148 right
Bust of the goddess Sekhmet in black granite.

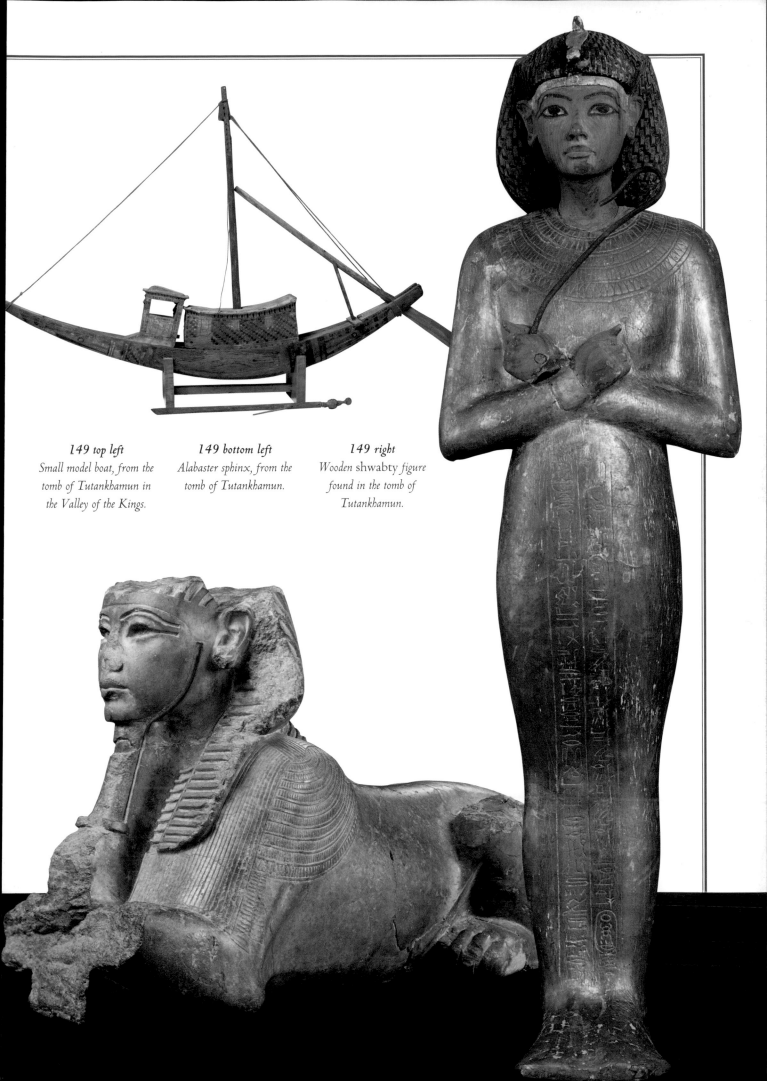

149 top left
Small model boat, from the tomb of Tutankhamun in the Valley of the Kings.

149 bottom left
Alabaster sphinx, from the tomb of Tutankhamun.

149 right
Wooden shwabty *figure found in the tomb of Tutankhamun.*

Western — Thebes —

T he kings of the Eighteenth, Nineteenth and Twentieth Dynasties built their tombs on the opposite side of Thebes, on the west bank of the Nile, in the silence of valleys hidden amidst the red and sun-baked mountains. Foregoing any form of external monumentality, they preferred multicolored internal decoration.

The choice of the lone valleys and the concealment of the entrances to the tombs with stones and detritus was evidently intended to avoid the already frequent violations. In the Valley of the Kings, religious tradition was satisfied by the western location of the tombs and underlined by the presence within the mountain range of an almost pyramidal peak, now known as al-Qurn. Visible from almost every point in the valleys, the peak was the petrification of the solar rays according to the symbolism of the Old and Middle Kingdoms.

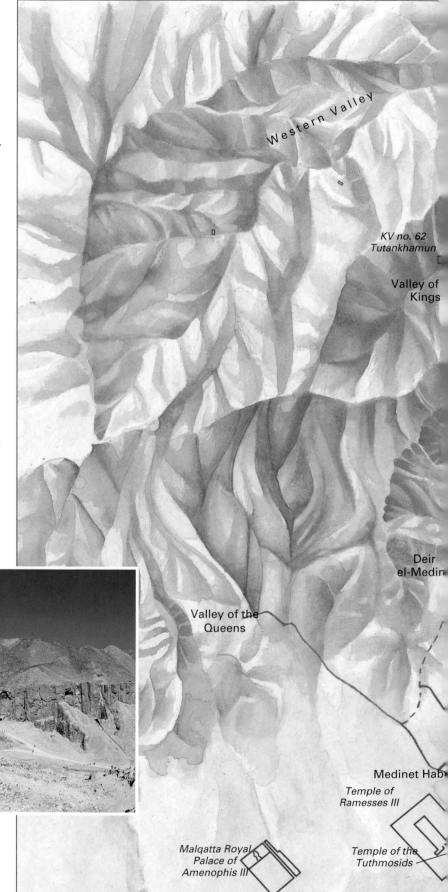

150 top
The burial chamber in the tomb of Tausert.

150 bottom
Panoramic view of the Valley of the Kings.

Tombs of Eleventh's Dynasty Nobles

Temple of Hatshepsut

Deir el-Bahri

Temple of Mentuhotep

El-Asasif

Dra Abu el-Naga

Mr Howard Carter's Residence

Sheikh Abd el-Qurna

Metropolitan Museum House

El-Khokhah

Upper Enclosure

Lower Enclosure

Temple of Sethos I

Qurna Village

*tolemaic Temple

Temple of Tuthmosis III

Temple of Amenophis II

Ramesseum

Temple of Tuthmosis IV

Temple of Nerneptah

Temple of Amenophis III

E.A.O. Office (Egyptian Antiquities Organizations)

Colossi of Memnon

The Temples — *of* — *Western Thebes*

154 top

Detail of the bas-reliefs that decorate the thrones of the Colossi of Memnon in which the personifications of Upper and Lower Egypt are depicted.

154 bottom

Aerial view of the Theban plain, with the Colossi of Memnon center-stage.

The pharaohs of the New Kingdom built their magnificent temples on the west bank of the Nile, at the edge of the cultivated land and in front of the Theban mountain. They all shared an east-west orientation.

The Theban temples had a different function to those of Giza and Saqqara that were constructed for funerary rituals and the cult of the pharaoh after his death. At Thebes instead, these buildings were intended to be used for the cult of the divine king while he was still alive and as memorials for the successive generations.

The magical rituals of the *Heb Sed* jubilee celebrations were conducted here on the occasion of the pharaoh's 30th year on the throne. An ancient tradition, they were intended to regenerate the spirit of the pharaoh and restore the vital energies crucial to the government and survival of the country.

154-155

*The Colossi of Memnon
once stood in front of the
pylon of the subsequently*

*destroyed funerary temple of
Amenhotep III. The overall
height of each statue is 58.7
feet.*

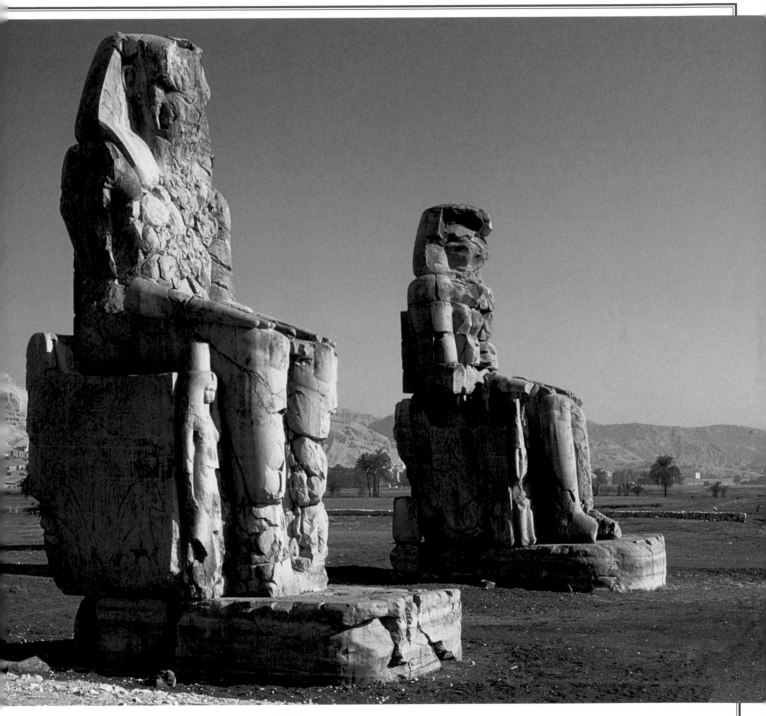

THE COLOSSI OF MEMNON

Memnon, the son of Aurora, is a figure in Greek mythology cited by Homer as the King of the Ethiopians, but had nothing to do with the two colossus statues named after him but portraying the pharaoh Amenhotep III. They dominate the entrance to a great temple of which nothing is left.

The colossi stand isolated on the plain one crosses to reach Medinet Habu and, standing around 60 feet high, they are imposing. They first became famous in the Roman era when, due to an earthquake, they cracked and as a result of thermal dilation and the morning breezes the northern colossus began to emit sounds similar to a lament, a phenomenon which the Greeks tried to explain as the god Memnon greeting his mother at dawn. The two statues were also situated on a very busy road that led to the south and had become a stopping-off place for the curious who rarely failed to leave evidence of their passing in the form of celebrated graffiti (over 100 examples have been found, including that of the emperor Hadrian).

156 top left
Lateral view of the great
hypostyle hall of the
Ramesseum.

156 bottom left
Granite head of one of the
statues of Rameses II that
adorned the Ramesseum.

156 right
The Osiris pillars and the
fragments of the colossal
statue of Rameses II in the
Ramesseum.

156-157
Aereal view of the
Ramesseum.

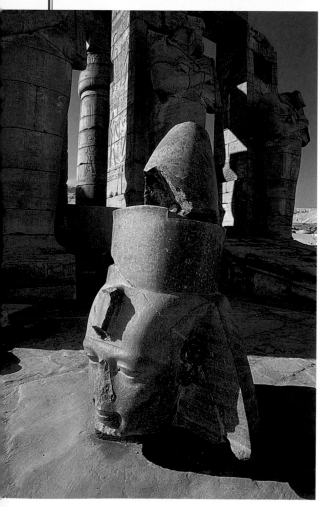

THE RAMESSEUM

The temple of Rameses II is part of a complex built by the pharaoh at Thebes West which included storerooms, enclosures for the temple materials, and homes for the servants of the temple. The imposing remains have been an attraction for travelers throughout the ages. The graffiti on the walls testify to the great number of visitors that have passed throughght, including Diodorus Siculus and G.B. Belzoni.

Commissioned by the British, in 1818 Belzoni succeeded in the arduous task of removing and shipping an enormous bust of the pharaoh which had lain since time immemorial in the courtyard in front of the temple and to send it to the British consul in Cairo, H. Salt. The bust was then moved to England and is today in the British Museum.

The plan of the site follows the classical layout: two successive courtyards, each preceded by a pylon, lead to a large hypostyle hall which in turn leads to a second, smaller hall in front of the shrine dedicated to Amun. The side walls of the temple feature Ramesside propaganda regarding the battle of Qadesh fought against the Hittites in present-day Syria. The relief sculptures show the four Egyptian armies involved in the battle and the king, depicted with giant-like proportions, who from his chariot wipes out entire platoons of minuscule enemies. There is an interesting sense of movement given to the scene through the representation of the horse's hooves, although in reality the Egyptian artists adopted this technique for different motives. They would repeatedly depict an object in order to indicate a plurality, an interpretation confirmed by careful examination of the animal's head where the faint outline of a second head can also be seen. Another significant detail, and one unique to the temples of Rameses, is the figure of Amun in the act of writing the pharaoh's name on a small tablet.

In front of the second pylon can be seen the remains of a huge statue of Rameses II. It probably cracked as a result of an earthquake—18th century drawings show it already in its present position. A project is currently under development to raise the statue to its original erect position, reassembling the various parts still scattered around the site.

157 center and bottom
The remains of the funerary
temple and a view of the chapel
of Amun in the temple of Sety I.

158-159
Ramesses II kneels in the
presence of Amun-Ra; from
a relief in the Ramesseum.

160-161
This view of the Ramesseum
reveals the size of the temple
enclosure.

THE TEMPLE OF SETY I

While requiring a slight diversion from the road leading to the Valley of the Kings, the temple of Sety I is well worth visiting. Many of the most beautiful buildings of the New Kingdom such as the temple at Abydos and the hypostyle hall at Karnak have been attributed to this pharaoh. Of the funerary temple at Western Thebes remains the covered temple, while the pylons and courtyards that once stood in front of it have been lost. Relief sculptures representing Sety I and Rameses II as children nursed respectively by Hathor and Mut reveal a regenerative significance in the building. The temple was principally consecrated to Amun, Ra-Horakty, the deified Rameses I, founder of the Nineteenth Dynasty, and the father of Sety I. However, the ruins also comprise areas dedicated to Atum and the warrior god Montu.

162-163

Ramesses II breaks through the
troops of Amurru defending the city of
Dapur in the Orontes valley; detail in
the Ramesseum.

164 top
Two columns stand in front of the pylon of the small temple of Thutmosis III.

164 bottom
Aerial view of Medinet Habu: the temple appears to be surrounded by a brick enclosure wall and is preceded by a fortified tower known as a migdol.

164-165
The first pylon of the temple of Medinet Habu, 207 feet long and decorated with bas-reliefs commemorating the victories of Rameses III.

165 bottom left
Black granite statue of the goddess Sekhmet, inside the complex.

165 bottom right
A section of the Osiris pylons surrounding the second courtyard.

THE SITE OF MEDINET HABU

During the Ramesside Period, Medinet Habu was an important economic and religious center and home to the pharaoh, the vizier, and the priests as well as the place from where the country was administered in the Twentieth Dynasty. It was moreover a site with ancient religious traditions as it was said to have been built on the hill where eight primordial divinities that existed prior to the creation of the world were buried and where the god Amun appeared for the first time.

The archaeological area comprises a temple from the Eighteenth Dynasty dedicated to Amun and built during the reign of Thutmosis III, the temple of Rameses III, the chapels of the worshippers of Amun, the small temple of Thot, the site of the royal palace

of Amenhotep III, the storerooms, the sacred lake, and nilometer. The whole complex was surrounded by a wall by Rameses III who wanted to render it similar to a fortress.

The temple of Rameses III is the site's most important monument, the Ramesseum being the inspiration for what was one of the most grandiose examples of Theban architecture.

The entrance comprises two massive pylons standing no less than 72 feet high and featuring sculpted military scenes including one of the king striking down with a mace a group of prisoners belonging to the subject peoples of Egypt, one with the pharaoh wearing the double crown and a sword sacrificing prisoners to Amun, and another of the pharaoh hunting the wild bull.

166
A view of the south portico in the first courtyard, with the large columns covered with multicolor bas-reliefs.

167 left
The pilasters of the portico in the second courtyard are decorated with scenes of offerings.

167 top right
Bas-relief sculpted on the southwest side of the first pylon depicting Rameses III hunting a bull.

167 center right
Detail of one of the bas-relief scenes decorating the walls of the first courtyard.

167 bottom right
Multicolor bas-relief with the winged solar disc, sculpted on one of the architraves of the second courtyard.

In the first great courtyard there is a portico with eight columns on one side and a gallery supported by Osirian pilasters and again decorated with battle scenes and offerings to the gods on the other.

The second pylon features bas-reliefs exalting military exploits with an abundance of details. There follows a second courtyard with Osirian pilasters and columns with closed capitals delineating a portico decorated with religious and military bas-reliefs.

From the courtyard one reaches the three hypostyle halls, of which the first had no less than 24 columns, and the inner sanctum that contained the sacred barque of Amun. The *sacellum* is flanked by the remains of two chapels dedicated to Mut and Khonsu and a short distance away is the chapel of Ra-Harmachis and that of the deified Rameses III himself. The external walls are all sculpted with bas-reliefs that continue to illustrate military exploits such as the naval battle with the sea peoples. An important element for scholars among the reliefs is a calendar listing the various religious festivities. Entering the temple today, one finds the following sequence of elements: a Roman courtyard from the imperial epoch, a Roman colonnade, a pylon from the era of Ptolemy IX and XII, the Nectanebo courtyard, and a pylon from the era of Shabaka. The original temple was begun by Amenhotep I and completed by Hatshepsut and Thutmosis III, as shown by certain figures and the cartouches found within the shrine. The consecrated part of the temple was then occupied during the Christian era by the Copts who left writings and paintings.

168-169
Aerial view of Deir al-Bahari, with the grandiose

temple of Hatshepsut and the adjacent temples of Thutmosis III and Mentuhotep.

168 bottom left
In this bas-relief, Queen Hatshepsut, portrayed with

male features, is offering a number of votive gifts to the falcon-headed god, Horus.

168 bottom right
A painted limestone sphinx
with the face of Hatshepsut,
found at Deir al-Bahari.

169 center
One of the friezes which best
preserves its colors depicts a
vulture surmounted by a
long series of ureaus.

169 left
View of the intermediate
portico, better known as the
"Portico of Punt."

169 bottom
Bas-relief depicting the god
Amun-Ra.

DEIR AL-BAHARI
THE TEMPLE OF HATSHEPSUT

Set in a spectacular natural amphitheater of
reddish rock, sacred to the goddess Hathor, stand
three temples that, when the sun is high in the sky
and the glare is dazzling, blend into the background
of rocky walls. This, the so-called Monastery of the
North, takes its name from the Coptic monastery
built a short distance away of which just a few ruins
remain today. The charisma of Queen Hatshepsut
has endured over the millennia, earning her a place
in the pantheon of great Egyptian sovereigns.
Research is still being conducted into her family ties
with Thutmosis II and Thutmosis III, while
fanciful hypotheses have been put forward regarding
her relationship with the architect Senmut. This last
was responsible for the construction of what is a
highly original temple. Despite being rebuilt,
virtually stone by stone, from the ruins first brought
to light by Naville in 1891, the building will never
match the spectacular magnificence of its past.

Originally, a gently rising monumental avenue
led towards the rocky amphitheater, flanked by
sphinxes and surrounded by gardens. The avenue
reached a first large courtyard with flower beds and
a colonnade interrupted by a second ramp leading
to the upper level. The wall of the portico was
decorated with bas-reliefs on a number of registers
with ritual scenes of hunting and fishing and the
ceremony of the erection of the obelisks in the
temple of Amun at Karnak. The second terrace
features two porticoes to the north (unfinished)
with 15 columns and four niches and a portico
with 44 square columns in a double row. To the left
is a chapel dedicated to Hathor and to the right
another dedicated to Anubis. Important bas-reliefs
rich in detail decorate the walls of the portico with
scenes from the life of the queen and the famous
expedition to the Land of Punt.

Climbing a ramp one reaches the portico of the
third terrace with 22 columns preceded by partially
reconstructed Osirian pilasters, while a pink granite
doorway leads into the hypostyle hall of which just

a few columns remain. On the left there are the two chapels dedicated to the royal cult of the queen and Thutmosis I while to the right is the one dedicated to the solar cult of Ra-Horakty. At the end of the hall is the entrance to the shrine of Amun where the sacred barque would once have been kept.

On the right of the third terrace is the chapel of Hathor composed of two hypostyle halls and other rooms and niches carved into the mountain and containing interesting bas-reliefs and the figure of the architect Senmut which appears a number of times behind the doors of certain niches.

Mention must be made of the deeply excavated tomb of Senmut, located close to the entrance to the first terrace. It contains a portrait of the architect while the ceiling features a representation of the constellations and the months of the year.

The tomb was never finished and Senmut was buried in the necropolis of Sheik Abd-al-Quarna, a fact that has alimented Egyptologists' studies and stimulated speculation about the queen and her vizier.

THE TEMPLE OF MENTUHOTEP I

The first of the temples to be built at Deir al-Bahari was the tomb of the first pharaoh of the Theban Eleventh Dynasty, Mentuhotep I who began the process of the unification of Egypt following the tormented First Intermediate Period.

The layout of the building was inspired by the temples of the Old Kingdom, to the extent that it resembled the funerary complex of Djoser and in part the sun temples of Abu-Sir. The texts of the Twelfth Dynasty called the temple "Akh-Sut-Nebhepetre" which means "Glorious are the places of Mentuhotep." The burial chamber is found in a subterranean grotto carved into the mountain at a depth of around 148 feet and is accessed via a descending corridor. Another tunnel leads to a crypt built as a cenotaph where Howard Carter discovered a painted sandstone statue that can now be seen in the Museum of Cairo. A pyramid with a base of around 66 feet probably once rose above the main building (mastaba). The design of the building was architecturally innovative both in terms of the access ramp to the terrace with walkways adorned with hexagonal columns forming a portico, and for the large hypostyle hall which was built with no less than 80 columns.

THE TEMPLE OF THUTMOSIS III

This tomb was discovered relatively recently (1962) as in its ruined state it had actually been overlooked. Bas-reliefs in limestone were discovered along with statues and graffiti left by the worshipers of the goddess Hathor. These relics are now conserved in the museums of Luxor and Cairo. The monument was built in the space between the rear hypostyle of the temple of Mentuhotep and the third terrace of the temple of Hatshepsut and was consecrated to Amun and Hathor. The temple also featured a large hall with 76 columns, a terrace, and an access ramp.

171 bottom left
The king and queen of Punt, the latter displaying signs of pathological obesity.

171 top right
One of the Hathoric capitals that adorn the columns of the chapel of Hathor.

171 bottom right
Another detail from the decorative scheme of the Portico of Punt, this time featuring two bearers.

172 top left
Detail of the burial chamber
in the tomb of
Tutankhamun.

172 center left
The southeast corner of the
vestibule in the tomb of
Horemheb.

The Theban Necropolises

THE VALLEY OF THE KINGS

Having left the green banks of the Nile and passed through the colorful villages, the road leads towards the rocky mountains rising behind Deir al-Bahari and penetrates a valley which itself branches into two further narrow and rugged valleys: the Valley of the Kings to the east, also known as the East Valley and identified by the code KV, and the Valley of the Monkeys or West Valley identified by the code WV.

The West Valley is not generally included in tourist itineraries due to the restricted number of tombs (four), only two of which (those of Amenhotep III and Ay) are open to the public. The Valley of the Kings instead houses 58 tombs identified with the KV code followed by the progressive number attributed on their discovery.

The area of Thebes West was conceived and utilized as a necropolis in the First Intermediate Period (2152-1994 B.C.) when three sovereigns of the Theban Eleventh Dynasty were buried there, beyond the west bank of the Nile at Al-Tarif. In the Middle Kingdom, the pharaoh Mentuhotep I had his tomb and funerary temple built in the stunning natural amphitheatre of Deir al-Bahari, the remains still being visible alongside the temple of Queen Hatshepsut. The oldest hypogean (subterranean) tombs in the Valley of the Kings appear to be KV 38 (attributed to Thutmosis I and built by the architect Ineni) and KV 20 built at the behest of Hatshepsut for herself and her father Thutmosis I (1504-1492 B.C.), while the last pharaoh to be buried in the valley was Rameses XI (1104-1075 B.C.).

172 bottom left
A view of the vestibule of the tomb of Horemheb, with the pharaoh before the gods.

172 right
Another detail of the wall paintings decorating the tomb of Horemheb.

173
The profusely decorated burial chamber of the tomb of Tutankhamun. It contains the magnificent pink quartzite sarcophagus which itself contains the first anthropoid coffin of the sovereign.

The tombs of the Theban valleys are all
hypogean and of the "syringe-type" as the Greeks
called them. The depth, the extension of the
excavations, and the subterranean configuration
varied from tomb to tomb (no two are identical) as
is demostrated by the composition of the tomb of
Tutankhamun (KV 62–just four rooms) compared
to that of Rameses II's children (KV 5–no less than
95). All of the rooms — stairways, corridors, halls
with colonnades, niches, and the funerary chamber
— are decorated with bright colors on tinted
backgrounds, according to the fashions of the period

in which they were built. Some of the tombs have
almost perfect frescos, others have been restored
with varying degrees of skill, while still others are
badly damaged and in some cases unfinished.
The latter should not be ignored as they allow
visitors to observe the techniques of painting and
bas-relief sculpture used by the ancient artists
and understand the stages in the artistic process.

The internal decoration, while being
different from one tomb to the next in pictorial
terms, was repetitive in the themes tackled. There
are always scenes of rituals and monotonous

176-177

*The rear wall of the burial
chamber of Ramesses I.*

178 top left
A detail of the colorful bas-reliefs in the tomb of Rameses III.

178-179
The spectacular burial chamber in the tomb of Sethnakht.

178 center left
Offering scene in the tomb of Rameses III.

179 bottom
The straight corridors leading to the burial chamber of the tomb of Merneptah.

178 bottom left
The great burial chamber in the tomb of Merneptah with the granite sarcophagus.

transcriptions of passages from sacred religious texts such as the *Book of the Dead* and the religious works of the New Kingdom. The aim was that of assisting the deceased on his journey through the underworld (*Am-Duat*). There are frequent representations of the solar barque with numerous deities overseeing the pharaoh's journey and protecting him from the evil spirits and the serpent Apophis.

The choice of tombs to visit is not free as the Egyptian authorities open the tombs in rotation so as to reduce the damage caused by the humidity brought in by the visitors. The entrance ticket to the valley generally includes entrance to three tombs (separate tickets can be purchased to visit the other tombs open at that time). It is suggested that you visit the following tombs, divided in three historical groups:

1st Period: KV 34 THUTMOSIS III
  KV 35 AMENHOTEP II
  KV 43 THUTMOSIS IV
2nd Period: KV 57 HOREMHEB
  KV 17 SETY I
  KV 8 MERNEPTAH
3rd Period: KV 11 RAMESES III
  KV 9 RAMESES VI

To this selection may be added the small tomb of Tutankhamun (KV 62) which only features decoration in the burial chamber containing the attractive sarcophagus in pink granite, with a second anthropomorphic sarcophagus in gilded wood containing the mummy of the young pharaoh. All of the funerary furnishings (3,500) found by Howard Carter in 1922 are in the Museum of Cairo.

181 bottom
*The burial chamber in the
tomb of Rameses VI
containing the sarcophagus
broken by thieves.*

180-181
*The astronomical ceiling of
the burial chamber in the
tomb of Rameses IX, with
the goddess Nut swallowing
the solar disc.*

180 bottom
*The magnificent sarcophagus
in red porphyry and detail
of the complex decorative scheme
of the tomb of Rameses IV.*

181 top
*Detail of the burial chamber of
the tomb of Rameses VI: the
solar disc is being lifted into the
sky by the goddess Nut.*

182-183

*The goddess of the sky, Nut, frames
the Book of the Night (bottom) and the Book
of the Day (top); from the tomb of Ramses VI.*

184-185
A view of the Valley of the Queens, the southernmost of the Theban necropolises.

184 bottom
The entrance to the tomb of Meritamun, the daughter and consort of Rameses II.

185 top
A detail of the ante-chamber in the tomb of Amun-her-khepshef, son of Rameses II.

185 bottom
Multicolor bas-relief in the burial chamber of the tomb of Ka-em-uaset.

186-187
The Valley of the Queens seems to be a vast indentation in the Libyan Desert.

THE VALLEY OF THE QUEENS

The Valley of the Queens is quickly reached after passing the Colossi of Memnon, leaving the temple of Medinet-Habu on the right and heading west for a mile.

Today the locality is known as Biban al-Harim but in ancient times it had the more appropriate and attractive name of "Ta-set-Neferu." While the compound place-name is difficult to translate, in the ancient Egyptian language the word *neferu* expressed a

subsequently abandoned due to the unstable terrain, many others were damaged by the rare but heavy rains, while still others were destroyed by Coptic religious vandals who built a monastery in the area, the ruins of which are still visible.

Despite its name, the valley was used for the burial not only of the queens, but also the sons and daughters of the kings and some court dignitaries, while in the Roman epoch even commoners were buried here. Research in the valley began following

concept of beauty found in numerous names that are associated in our collective imagination with the perfection of queens such as Nefertiti and Nefertari.

As with the Valley of the Kings, the site chosen for the tombs was protected by the pyramidal mountain al-Qurn and, moreover, according to some authorities, the natural cavern eroded by flood waters at the bottom of the valley might have represented a divine uterus from which the deceased buried in the valley could be reborn. Evidence of around a hundred tombs has been found in the Valley of the Queens. Work on many of these began but was

the Franco-Tuscan expedition organized by Champollion and Rosellini in 1829, although Belzoni had entered the valley in 1816, leaving graffiti on the entrance to the tomb of Tyti. There followed Lepsius, Brugsch, and finally the expedition of 1903 led by Schiapparelli who brought to light all of the most important tombs visible today, including the tomb of Nefertari, Rameses II's "great royal bride," which is considered the best in the valley and one of the greatest of all the Theban tombs. The tombs in this Valley, all from the Eighteenth, Nineteenth, Twentieth and Twenty-first Dynasties, are identified with the code QV.

188 and 189

All the images on these pages reproduce details of the sumptuous decorative scheme adorning the walls of the tomb of Nefertari, discovered by Ernesto Schiapparelli in 1904 and subjected to a long and complex restoration completed in 1992.

THE TOMB OF NEFERTARI (QV 66)

Nefertari (Nofretari-Mery-am-Mut) was the favorite wife of Rameses II. Never before in Egypt had a queen been held in such high regard by a pharaoh who, in her honor, ordered the construction of a temple at Abu Simbel alongside his own and the excavation of a tomb worthy of a sovereign. This tomb is the most beautiful and most richly decorated in the Valley of the Queens.

The origins of Nefertari are not absolutely clear. She was probably born into a noble Theban family and may have been related in some way to Ay, the successor to Tutankhamun in 1323 B.C. She married Rameses II before his coronation and had five or six children with him. We know little about Nefertari's death other than the fact that after the jubilee marking the thirtieth anniversary of Rameses II's reign, her name no longer appeared in the inscriptions and thus she may have died around 1250 B.C. at an age of around 40/45 years.

The tomb was discovered by Ernesto Schiapparelli in 1904 during the first systematic search of the Valley of the Queens performed by the Italian Archaeological Mission. It was closed to the public for many years to avoid damaging the paintings with restoration work that began in 1988 being completed in 1992. Since then the subterranean tomb has been reopened but only for a restricted number of visitors which means tickets need to be booked in advance.

The plan of this tomb is more complex than those of the others in the valley and was derived from the examples in the Valley of the Kings. Following the first flight of stairs from the entrance the sequence of rooms is as follows: antechamber, vestibule and annexe, a second flight of steps leading to the burial chamber with two annexes,

190 and 191
The tomb of Nefertari, with its very complex plan and sumptuous decorative scheme is considered to be one of the most beautiful in the Valley of the Queens. In order to preserve the splendor of the delicate decoration, access to the tomb has been drastically restricted.

192-193
Hathor - She who presides over Thebes, and the Lady of the Sky - welcomes Ramesses II's bride Nefertari; sarcophagus room, southwest pillar.

and a cell. Specialist texts should be consulted for a more detailed description, but the following information may suffice for ordinary visitors.

The ceilings are fairly low compared with those of other tombs and are all painted a deep blue and decorated with gold five-pointed stars as seen in a number of tombs in the Valley of the Kings. The solid rectangular section pilasters are decorated with divinities and frequently the *djed* symbol with the cartouches and titles of the queen. The walls are in turn decorated with excerpts from the *Book of the Dead*, with texts and figures illustrating the journey of the queen's spirit as she descends to the underworld before being reborn as a deity.

194 top left
The interior of the Ptolemaic temple at Deir al-Medina.

194 bottom left
The restored interior of the same tomb.

194 center left
The entrance to the tomb of Ipui at Deir al-Medina.

194 right
A view of the workers' village of Deir al-Medina.

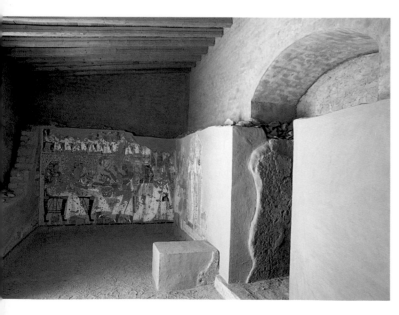

THE SITE OF DEIR AL-MEDINA

Deir al-Medina is close to the Valley of the Queens and less than a mile from the Valley of the Kings. It was from here that the footpaths followed by the workers excavating and decorating the royal tombs departed.

Today we find the remains of the workers' village, the tombs of the craftsmen cut into the mountainside and a small temple from the Ptolemaic era dedicated to Hathor-Maat and later used by Coptic Christians as a monastery. Founded and inhabited from the Eighteenth Dynasty onwards, when construction began in the Valley of the Kings with the tomb of Thutmosis I, the village has a rectangular plan and occupies a surface area of around 70,000 square feet. At the height of its expansion it could accommodate around 700 people.

Local excavations have brought to light the foundations of houses, the layout of the streets and a wealth of relics that have allowed, a relatively rare occurrence, the everyday lives of ordinary families to be reconstructed.

The necropolis of Deir al-Medina was built on the slopes of the hill overlooking the village to the west and comprises over 400 tombs from the Nineteenth and Twentieth Dynasties, of which only 53 are frescoed.

The local tombs typically feature an imposing entrance with pylons similar to a miniature temple, an internal courtyard leading to the chapel, and a shaft or a steep flight of steps down to the funerary chamber cut into the rock. The chapels were frequently surmounted externally by a small pyramid in unfired bricks.

The interiors and, in particular, the burial chambers, were richly frescoed in bright colors,

194-195 e
195 bottom left
A panoramic view of the temple of Deir al-Medina and the necropolis.

195 bottom right
The interior of the tomb of Khabekhnet, a functionary at the time of Rameses II, with the two fragmentary

statuary groups representing the deceased's parents (to the left of the door) and the deceased himself with his consort (right).

196-197
General view of the village and necropolis of the workers at Deir al-Medina.

195

198 *top left*
The northeast wall of the tomb of Sennegem, on which the sacred Fields of Iaru in the underworld, are depicted.

198 *bottom left*
A view of the sumptuous interior of the tomb of Pashedu, with a scene where he is drinking at a spring.

while the funerary chambers and annexes contained furnishings, objects, and foods intended for use in the underworld.

The most tombs of greatest interest are the following.

Senegem (TT 1)

A necropolis functionary at the time of Sety I and Rameses II, Senegem's tomb is frescoed on an ochre background with scenes of religious ceremonies and everyday life in excellent condition. The tomb was found virtually intact and all the furnishings are conserved in the Museum of Cairo.

Pashedu (TT 3)

Necropolis functionary and chief painter of the tomb of Sety I.

Ipuy (TT 217)

Chief sculptor of the necropolis, Ipuy's house in the village has also been identified. The tomb features interesting scenes depicting everyday life (agriculture, trade, boat-building, weaving, and so on).

Inherkhaon (TT 359)

Inherkhaon was defined as "foreman of the lord of the two lands in the plaza of truth" and worked for Rameses II and IV during the Twentieth Dynasty.

The crypt is composed of two vaulted chambers brightly painted with figures from the *Book of the Dead*.

198 right
The wife of Pashedu,
Negemtebehdet, portrayed in
the style typical of the
Ramesside Period.

198-199
The magnificent interior of
the tomb of Sennegem, a
functionary who lived at the
time of Sety I.

200-201

Sennedjem and his consort
Iyneferti are shown during
the plowing, seeding, and
harvesting of their crops in

the Fields of Iaru, the
Egyptian version of paradise.

202-203

In the paintings on the vault

of Sennedjem's burial
chamber, the deceased is
shown, sometimes with his
wife, worshiping various
gods and goddesses.

204-205

In this scene in the tomb of
Pashedu, Osiris is shown
seated wearing the royal
nemes headdress.

206 top and center top
The entrance and the hypostyle hall of the monumental tomb of Ramose, a high ranking dignitary at the time of Amenhotep IV.

206 bottom center
A detail of a wall painting in the tomb of Ramose.

206 bottom
Preparatory drawing for a never completed painting in the tomb of Ramose.

206-207
A detail of the interior of the tomb of Panehesi.

207 bottom left
A painting in the tomb of Nekhtamun.

207 bottom right
View of the sumptuous tomb of Neferronpet.

THE NECROPOLIS OF SHEIKH ABD-EL-QURNA

Between Deir al-Medina and the hilly area to the west of the temple of Sety I lie over 500 tombs of high ranking functionaries and notables from the Eighteenth Dynasty (the Tombs of the Nobles), grouped in a number of necropolises named according to their locations. The most representative site is that of Sheikh Abd-el-Qurna, located on a terrace between Deir al-Medina and Deir al-Bahari and comprising many well preserved tombs. The local tombs are not very large and are generally composed of an open courtyard, a vestibule in which the titles of the deceased are found, and a corridor leading to the burial chamber with niches. These tombs feature more down-to-earth subjects than the religious symbolism of the royal tombs in the Valley of the Kings, a difference similar to that between the images in the mastabas and those typical of the funerary monuments of the Old Kingdom. The paintings boast magnificent colors and are extremely attractive, but are also remarkable for the joyful serenity with which life is represented within a funerary setting. Only around thirty of the tombs are open to visitors and an inevitable selection should be made from among the following:

Sennefer (TT 96): mayor of the City of the South (Amenhotep II)

Khaemhat (TT 57): Royal Scribe and Inspector of the Granaries (Amenhotep III)

Khonsu (TT 31): First Prophet of Men-kheper-ra (Thutmosis I)

Rekhmire (TT 100): Vizier and Governor of the City (Thutmosis III - Amenhotep II)

Menna (TT 69): Scribe of the Land Register (Thutmosis IV)

Nakht (TT 52): Scribe-Astronomer of Amun (Thutmosis IV)

Paser (TT 106): Vizier and Governor of the Valley (Sety I - Rameses II)

Haremhab (TT 78): Royal Scribe (Thutmosis III - Amenhotep III)

Kenamon (TT 93): Chief Intendent to the King (Amenhotep III)

Ramose (TT 55): Vizier and Governor of the City (Amenhotep IV)

208-209
The tomb of Khaemhat is one of the few non-royal tombs in the necropolis at Thebes to be decorated with reliefs.

210-211
Ramose, the governor of the city and vizier during the reign of Amenhotep IV, had a proper 'palace of eternity' built at the foot of the Sheikh Abd el-Qurna hills.

Esna

Esna is located 36 miles to the south of Luxor, on the left bank of the Nile and over the ruins of the city of Latopolis. It was a prosperous trading center during the New Kingdom thanks to its geographical position at the convergence of the roads linking the Nile valley with the cities of the south.

The principal deity venerated at Esna was the ram-headed god Khnum, a creator who modeled every animal and plant on his potter's wheel. The Temple of Esna is dedicated to this divinity and the goddess Neith who was represented as a lates fish (*latus niloticus*, hence the name Latopolis). The temple—transformed in to a Christian church and used as a storeroom for cotton in more recent times—was discovered by Champollion in 1828, and was actually a reconstruction from the reign of Ptolemy VI in the first century A.D. of a building from the Eighteenth Dynasty. It is located in the heart of the city, below street level. All that remains of the temple built during the reigns of Tiberius, Claudius, and Vespasian is a large hypostyle hall measuring 108 feet by 54 feet, with 24 columns

212 top
A view of the interior of the large hypostyle hall, the ceiling of which is supported by 18 columns.

212 bottom
The cross-pieces that link the columns of the facade are profusely decorated with bas-reliefs.

213 top
This bas-relief on one of the
internal columns shows the
emperor Trajan offering
lotus flowers to the god
Khnum.

213 bottom
The capitals inside the
hypostyle hall are
characterized by a lively
color scheme.

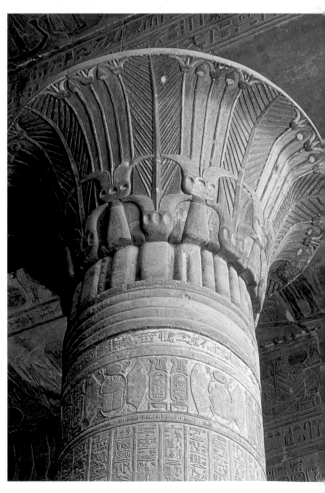

212-213
*The large hypostyle hall—an
excellent example of the
religious architecture of the
Ptolemaic Period—is all that
remains of the temple
consecrated to the ram-
headed god, Khnum.*

with magnificent capitals decorated with floral
motifs. The last hieroglyphs to be carved in the
temple date from the middle of the third century A.D.,
as do the mural decorations with symbolic images of
the fraticidal struggle between the Roman emperors.
Linked to those of the ceiling depicting the zodiac,
the constellations and the course of the sun
underline the concept that the entire universe is
enclosed within the temple and that it was built in
accordance with the laws of the cosmos.

The back wall features two unusual inscriptions,
hymns to the god Khnum. The first is composed
exclusively of the hieroglyphic symbol for the
crocodile, the second of the hieroglyphic symbol for
the ram.

214 top
The statue of Horus in the form of a falcon set before the entrance to the hypostyle hall.

214 bottom
The facade of the first hypostyle hall features six columns united at the bottom by decorated cross-pieces.

214-215
The temple of Edfu, of which the 154-foot high entrance pylon is seen here, is considered to be one of the best preserved in all Egypt.

215 bottom left
One of the bas-reliefs decorating the peripheral corridor shows the pharaoh receiving the double crown.

215 bottom right
The replica of the solar boat built by Mariette in the late nineteenth century is conserved in one of the internal halls.

Edfu

E dfu, known to the ancients as Hebau, is situated around 60 miles south of Luxor, on the west bank of the Nile. It was the capital of the second *nome* of Upper Egypt, an important and wealthy city since the Old Kingdom, and the home of Horus, the celestial god represented by the falcon whose wings symbolize the extension of the cosmos. The temple dedicated to this deity is remarkably well preserved, probably thanks to the long period during which it was buried beneath the desert sands. Only the upper parts of the building allowed the French expedition of 1798 to identify the site and it was not until 1860 that Auguste Mariette, then the director of the Service des Antiquités Egyptiennes, began work to free it from the sands.

The building as we see it today is virtually intact and in terms of size is the second largest Egyptian temple after Karnak and the largest of the monuments dedicated to Horus. Work on the temple began in 237 B.C. during the reign of Ptolemy III and was finished in 57 B.C., under Ptolemy XII.

The temple is entered via the monumental portal set between the two towers of the pylon. Above this portal is a balcony from which once a year during a solemn ritual, the priests presented the falcon chosen to embody the living god (to this end a school of falconry was established at Edfu).

Having passed the two towers, one enters a courtyard bound on three sides by a colonnade, with the entrance to the first hypostyle hall at the far end. This hall contains one of the most imposing statues of Horus ever sculpted, whereas at the sides are two small chambers, the House of the Morning, which celebrates rising of the sun and symbolizes the faith required to enter to the temple, and the House of Books on the left which gave access to sacred knowledge. Beyond the first hall is a second, smaller hypostyle hall with 12 columns which in turn communicates with three chambers: the first on the right is the so-called "treasure chamber" and conserves the names of the mineral-rich regions annexed by Egypt, on the left is the room of the Nile bringing prosperity, and the Laboratory with inscribed recipes for perfumes and unguents used in religious ceremonies.

The second hall leads to the offerings chamber and is linked via roof to a central chamber. On the left of this last is a chapel dedicated to the god Min, while to the right is a small courtyard with an altar and chapel used as a vestibule.

Inside the central chamber or *naos* is the true

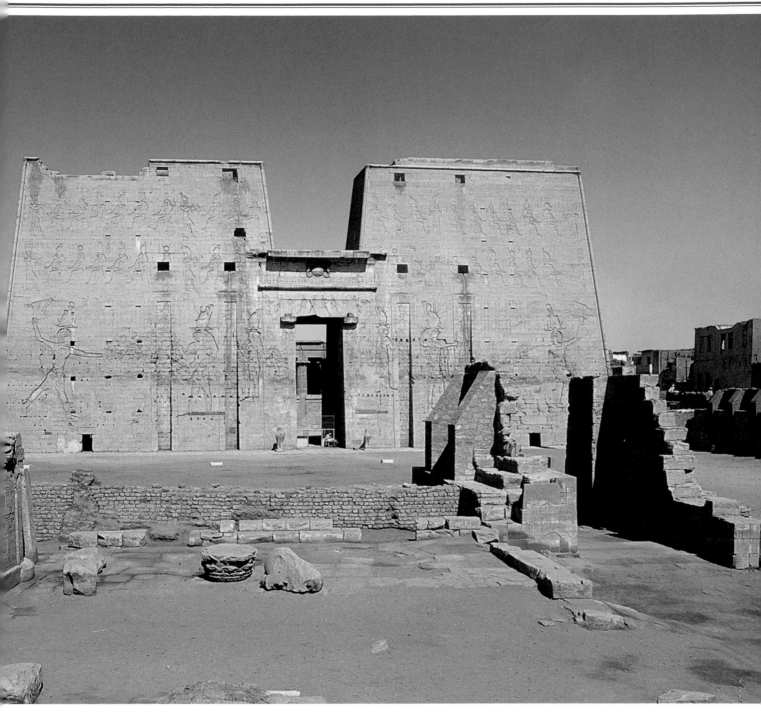

inner sanctum, a temple within a temple containing
an altar housing a statue of the god, surrounded by a
corridor with chapels in which scenes of the Horus
legend are inscribed.

Daily worship took the form of three services:
one in the morning with offerings of food by the
priest who entered the *naos* and, in the presence of the
statue, fed its power before closing the door of the
naos and eliminating evidence of his passing by walking
backwards; the second was at midday, when the *naos*
remained closed but aspersions and fumigations were
performed; the last service was held in the evening
and consisted of a ritual of offerings and purification
through incense. At Edfu a typical feature of temple
architecture can be seen in the symbolic succession of
spaces that are ever smaller and darker.

Kom Ombo

Kom Ombo, or the city of gold, known to the ancient Greeks and Egyptians as Ombos and Nubit respectively, is situated on the right bank of the Nile, around 30 miles from Aswan. Thanks to its strategic position above a promontory from which it was easy to survey the river traffic, Kom Ombo became a site of primary importance for the Egyptian army, allowing it to set a second stronghold on the Nile after Aswan.

The city nonetheless remained essentially a center of agriculture and trade with Nubia, above all throughout the Ptolemaic Period. Building work on the temple began during the reign of Ptolemy VI, was completed under Ptolemy XII, and was based on the remains of a shrine dating back to the Eighteenth Dynasty and brought to light during excavations conducted in 1893.

The building is dedicated to two deities, Sobek, the crocodile god, and Haroeris (Horuis the Elder), the falcon god. In this case Sobek is identified as the evil Seth, the enemy of Horus. The temple features a great number of crocodiles as the Egyptians believed that by transforming them into religious icons they would be spared by the fearsome reptiles. Many examples were kept in

captivity and mummified on their death.

Of the Ptolemaic temple, only part of the curtain wall, a number of columns, a few sections of the *pronao* and the chapels, and a *mammisi* have survived. The entrance is constituted by the pylon forming part of the monumental portal, with twin doors for Sobek and Horus, of which little remains. To the south of the great courtyard, on the right of the temple, is a chapel dedicated to the goddess Hathor containing numerous crocodile mummies. Beyond the pylon lies the courtyard delimited by now ruined colonnades and featuring a sacrificial altar in the center. From here one reaches the first of the hypostyle halls with twin entrances which had the function of purifying the pharaoh by both Horus and Thot in the presence of the temple deities Sobek and Haroeris.

The two conflicting deities are obliged to co-operate in the struggle against the forces of darkness. This dualism is also seen in the architectural layout, with the following arrangement of the elements composing the complex: two entrances, two corridors surrounding the *naos*, dual passages between the various parts of the building, and the inner sanctum divided into two shrines. In the context of this dualism the two deities are consecrated not so much separately as integral parts of each other. The second hypostyle hall, smaller than the first, boasts walls decorated with numerous hieroglyphs concerning the rules and

217 bottom
The front of the well
preserved chapel of Hathor,
erected by the

emperor Domitian, in
which the mummies of the
sacred crocodiles are
conserved.

218-219
The two entrances of the temple
at Kom Ombo lead to the
sanctuaries of Haroeris and Sobek.

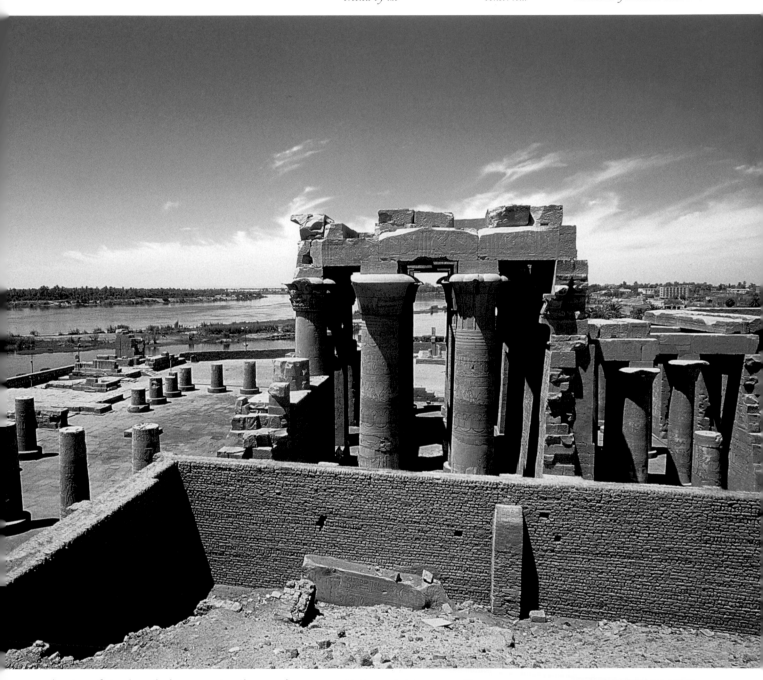

conduction of rituals with the respective places and
dates. Three halls anticipate the inner sanctum. In the
first, the pharaoh lays the foundations of the temple.
The second, known as the Hall of Offerings, gives
access to the roof where at the beginning of each year
the ritual of union with the solar disc was celebrated.
During this ritual the statues of the deities (kept in
the third hall) were exposed to the light of the new
year in order to absorb positive energy. At the heart
of the three halls lies the inner sanctum, probably
once divided into two parts separated by a wall, with
the area dedicated to Haroeris on the left and on the
right, that of Sobek.

Aswan

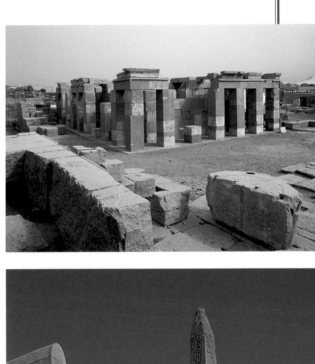

A swan, known in ancient times as Syene, is situated in an enchanting natural setting that makes it one of the most inviting attractions in the whole of Egypt. The lush vegetation mitigates the high temperatures brought by the warm winds from the desert, while the Nile, here divided by Elephantine Island, seems more blue than further down the valley. A point of departure for visits to the Nubian temples, Aswan offers a number of archaeological attractions including the ruins on the Island of Elephantine, once the capital of the first and southernmost *nome* of Egypt. Here, in the welcome shade of sycamore trees, is the entrance to the famous Nilometer, partially rebuilt in the Roman epoch and carrying inscriptions dating from the reigns of Thutmosis III, Amenhotep III (Eighteenth Dynasty) and Psamtek II (Twenty-sixth Dynasty). In all probability, however, its construction dates back to even earlier times. Still on the island, further excavations have brought to light a late temple of Khnum (Thirtieth Dynasty) and the temple of Satet, his female counterpart (Eighteenth Dynasty). On the southern tip of the island is a Ptolemaic temple rebuilt using blocks of stone belonging to the foundations of the temple of Kalabsha. Crossing the river by felucca and landing on the western bank, one may visit the subterranean tombs dug into the mountains by the princes of Elephantine, their long, steep access stairs visible from the town. There are notable tombs belonging to Sirenput I and Sirenput II, both the first superintendent of the priests of Khnum and Satet and governor of Aswan. Following a rapid visit to the Christian monastery St. Simeone, established in the seventh century and rebuilt in the tenth century, the quarries to the north of the city, where the Egyptians extracted rock for their monumental buildings and obelisks, are undoubtedly worthy of close inspection. An unfinished example of the latter was abandoned in the quarry after the stone cracked. Nearby a museum houses relics mainly found in Nubia.

221 center

The remains of the temple of Satet on Elephantine Island.

221 bottom

The obelisk at the entrance of the Archaeological Museum on Elephantine comes from Abu Simbel.

222-223

Elephantine lies on ancient Egypt's southern border and has many ruins.

Philae

S ituated to the south of Aswan, the monumental complex of Philae features the largest of the temples dedicated to Isis. Built during the third century B.C., this was the last bastion of ancient Egyptian religion, the place in which the last hieroglyphs were inscribed, in 437 A.D. It long remained the only temple in which the Egyptian priests could still perform the old rites in a period in which Christianity was spreading. In 535 the Roman emperor Justinian had the temple closed definitively. The scribes and the priests were exiled, the doors to the inner sanctum were forced, and the temple fell into the hands of the Christian hermits who devastated it. The *naos* was profaned and the hypostyle hall became a Christian church.

The need for a reservoir to meet the demand for irrigation water during the seasons in which the Nile is at its lowest led to the construction in the late nineteenth century of the first dam at Aswan. This was little short of disastrous for the ancient monuments which were thus submerged for much of the year. Then, in 1960, a new threat appeared in the form of work on the construction of a second dam (that created Lake Nasser). On completion of the Aswan High Dam the temple complex would have been permanently submerged to a depth of 13 feet.

Between 1972 and 1980 the buildings at Philae were saved in a remarkable operation involving their transfer to the nearby island of Agilka. Each individual stone was numbered and its position noted so as to allow a faithful reconstruction of the monuments. The operation lasted almost 10 years and in 1980 Philae (or rather the transformed Agilka) was finally reopened to the public.

In antiquity the region represented the interface between the Egyptians and the Nubian peoples. This explains the presence at Philae of shrines

224 bottom
The gateway to the Abaton,
rebuilt by Ptolemy III on the
island of Biga.

224-225
The landing place, on Biga,
near which are the kiosk and
the obelisk of Nectanebo.

225 bottom
The Kiosk of Trajan,
erected by the Roman
emperor in 105 A.D.

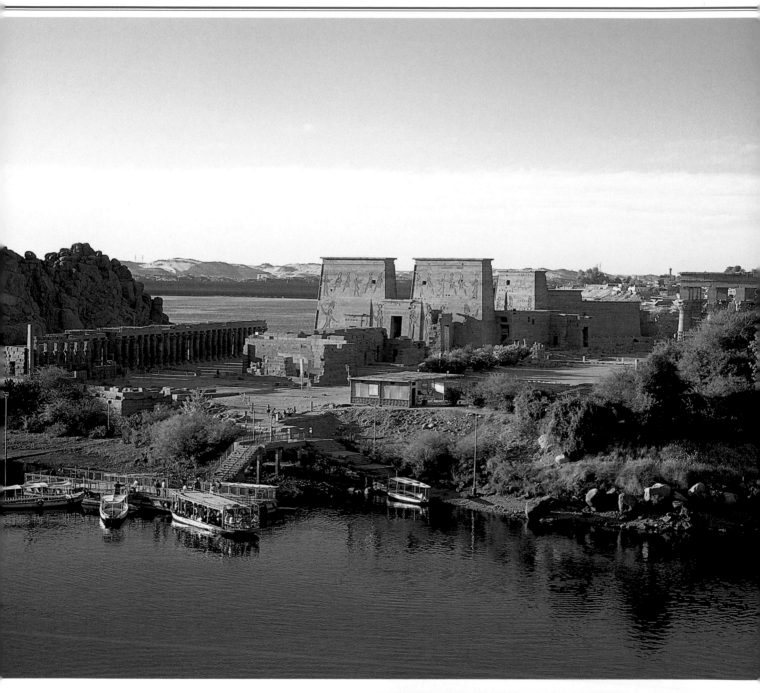

dedicated to certain deities. During the centuries preceding the expansion of Christianity, the cult of the goddess Isis enjoyed unrivaled popularity that went well beyond the Egyptian borders and was to lead, particularly during the first centuries of the present era, to the erection of sacred buildings dedicated to the goddess in the Roman empire.

The Philae complex is a group of temples, the largest of which is dedicated to the goddess Isis and characterized by an apparent disorder in the elements of which it is composed. Each is set on its own axis and has its own direction, the colonnades are not

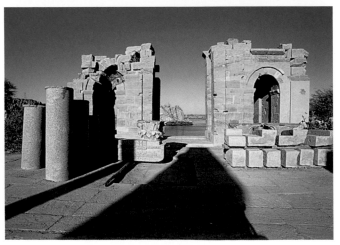

parallel but each section has its raison d'être. Isis is the goddess that embodied life itself, and as life is not rational, neither is it symmetrical or parallel.

The landing on the island is to the south, alongside the pavilion of Nectanebo I. From here one passes through two portals opening in a "V" and giving access to the temple of Isis. On the east side of the island is the kiosk of Trajan (rebuilt by the emperor with reliefs illustrating him making offerings to the gods) which housed the barque of Isis used during the processions. Still on the east side, close to the principal temple is the small temple dedicated to the goddess Hathor.

A large paved area precedes the first pylon of the temple of Isis with two tall blocks on either side of a small doorway. Having passed the first pylon, one enters a large courtyard, on the west side of which is a free-standing building, the *mammisi*, a temple symbolizing birth in which Isis delivered her son Horus. The east side is instead occupied by a portico housing six small chambers.

The second pylon gives access to the closed area of the temple, behind which is a hall with ten columns. This is a cosmic site, with mythical and astrological decoration linked to the laws of the sky of Isis. Understanding of the rules of sacred astrology was an indispensable condition for access to the twelve-roomed *naos* (each one representing a zodiac sign). The temple also features a crypt and, on the roof, a chapel for the veneration of the god Osiris (Isis's consort), with scenes of the ritual in which Osiris is dead and the king intervenes with the deities to allow the god's spirit to continue to live. Osiris is revived, darkness and death are defeated, and the love and faith of Isis triumph over destiny.

In front of the island of Philae lies that of Biga which housed the Abaton, the tomb of Osiris. Today little remains of the temple which once stood there.

226-227
The gateway that opens in the first pylon, preceded by two lions installed during the late Roman Period.

226 bottom
In the Roman Period the Diocletian gateway was the main entrance to the island.

227 top
A view of the kiosk of Nectanebo, with the Hathoric capitals on its columns, and the neighboring obelisk.

227 center
A perspective view of the eastern colonnade, much of which remains unfinished.

227 bottom
The bas-reliefs sculpted on the first pylon show the goddess Isis and the god Horus, the features of which were unfortunately partially obliterated by Coptic monks when the temple was transformed into a Christian church.

The Nubian Temples

Wadi as-Sebua, Amada, Derr, and Quertassi. These ancient monuments were unknown to modern travellers until recently and are four of the eleven archaeological sites in lower Nubia (the ancient Wawat) to survive the inundation caused by the construction of the new dam at Aswan.

Fortunately, many other sites were excavated and examined before the water submerged them forever, and the most important were dismantled and reconstructed on alternative sites safe from the rising tide. Only in recent years has the introduction of cruises to the region allowed hundreds of visitors to view the monuments each day.

NEW KALABSHA, QERTASSI, BEIT AL-WALI

Three temples have been grouped not far from the Philae complex, in the New Kalabsha area around a half mile south of the Aswan High Dam. They were originally situated within a radius of 30 miles from the present site.

The Kalabsha temple, defined by Maspero as "the most beautiful in Nubia," was rebuilt in the age of Augustus in the Ptolemaic style and was consecrated to the cult of the deity Mandulis, the Nubian version of the Egyptian god Horus. It is composed of a pylon, a courtyard with porticoes on three sides, a hypostyle hall with twelve columns, two vestibules, and a shrine. The transfer from the original site brought to light pre-existing structures from the periods of Amenhotep II and Ptolemy IX. The unfinished temple has a number of interesting features such as depictions of Augustus in the guise of a pharaoh, making offerings to Egyptian deities, and Greek inscriptions relating to the Nubian king Silko who, in the fifth century B.C., commemorated his victory of the rival desert tribes. Close to the site is the kiosk of Kertassi, composed of four intact columns clearly dating from the Ptolemaic Period.

WADI AS-SEBUA, DAKKA, AND MAHARRAKA

A desolate, arid, desert land, enclosed by granite mountains dusted with a red sand that at times takes on yellowish tones is the panorama that divides New Kalabsha from the second Nubian temple site, around 68 miles away, a day's journey by boat. During this silent voyage one passes over the temple of Gerf Hussein, now completely submerged by the water. Internally

228 top
The elegant and minute kiosk of Kardassy, reconstructed near the temple of Kalabsha.

228 center
The small rock temple of Beit al-Whali, also rebuilt at New Kalabsha.

228 bottom
The innermost hall of the rock temple of Beit al-Whali, supported by massive protodoric columns.

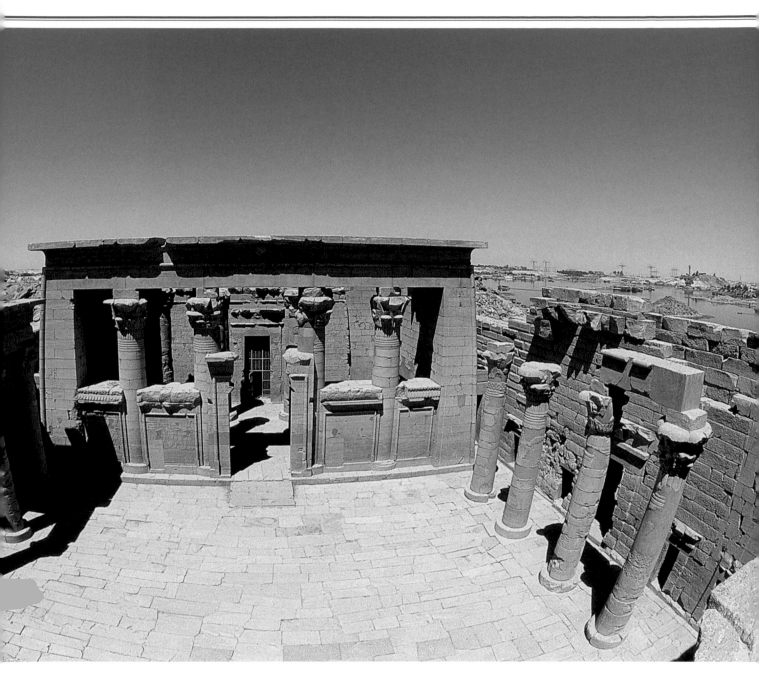

the monument was similar to the temple at Abu Simbel but could not be saved due to the friable nature of the rock from which it had been carved.

One lands at New Sebua where one may admire the temples of Al Dakka, Maharraka, and Wadi as-Sebua. This last name, which means in Arabic the "valley of the lions," derives from the sphinxes that adorn the entrance to the temple. The building was erected at the behest of Rameses II and dedicated to the veneration of the god Amun Horakty. The interior features depictions of offerings that were continuously made to the deities in these religious sanctuaries. This site too was restored by the The Copts who transformed it into a Christian church. There is an interesting depiction of St Peter offering flowers to the "powerful bull, king of Upper and Lower Egypt," Rameses II. The complex was moved just 3 miles from its original site, with the sphinxes already partially submerged in a desperate race against time.

The temple of Dakka, originally situated 25 miles to the north of its present position, dates from the Ptolemaic and Roman Periods. Dedicated to Thot, the temple was built by Ptolemy IV and Arqamani, King of Meroe (circa 200 B.C.), with part of the site covering the remains of older buildings. Further additions were made by Ptolemy VIII and the Roman emperor, Augustus.

In the vicinity of Dakka is Maharaqq, the third temple in the group, located around 20 miles from its original position. Of reduced dimensions and unfinished, the temple was dedicated to the cult of the Ptolemaic god, Serapis.

228-229
The facade of the hypostyle hall in the temple of Kalabsha. This complex consecrated to the god Mandulis was built during the Ptolemaic Period and is considered to be the most grandiose Nubian monument after Abu Simbel.

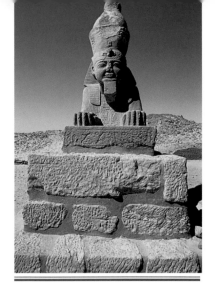

230 top left
The Osiris pylon that
delimit the long sides of the
courtyard in the temple of
Wadi Sabua.

230 left center top
The temple of Amada,
begun by Thutmosis III
and completed by
Amenhotep II.

230 left center bottom
The well conserved pylon of
the temple of Dakke.

AMADA, DERR, AND THE TOMB OF PENNIUT I

The third site is around 30 miles away at Amada, the name being taken from that of the oldest of the structures rebuilt here, the temple of Amada, dedicated to Amun and Ra-Horakty. Built by the Thutmosis III (Eighteenth Dynasty) and subsequently extended by Thutmosis IV during the Amarnian Period, the temple was dedicated to the cult of Amun before being restored to the traditional deities under Sety I. It was later transformed into a Christian church by the Copts. The colored relief sculptures complicated the removal operation. Almost two miles of rails were laid on which the temple, fixed to steel frames, was transported to the present site, overcoming a difference in height of over 197 feet.

The temple of Derr, completely carved out of the rock, was dedicated to the cult of Ra-Horakty and was built at the behest of Rameses II. It was rebuilt over six miles from its original site.

The rock tomb of Penniut I, built by a local governor during the reign of Rameses VI, completes the site.

230 bottom left
The "Feasting Hall" in the
underground temple at
Derr.

230 right
One of the sphinxes of the
dromos at Wadi Sabua.

230-231
The splendid temple of Wadi
Sebua, preceded by the
avenue of sphinxes.

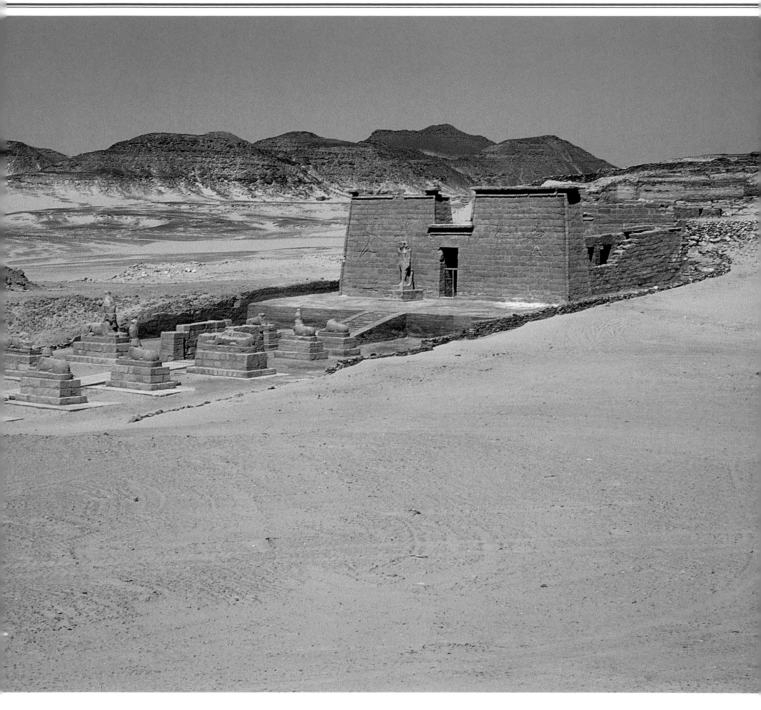

QASR IBRIM

The city-fortress of Qasr Ibrim, once set around 200 feet above the level of the Nile, now has to cope with the waters of the lake lapping its foundations. Built by the Nubians following the withdrawal of the Egyptians in around 900 B.C., it was restored on a number of occasions and extended by the Romans. Subsequently inhabited by the Copts, it was occupied by the Mamlukes fleeing from Ishmael Pasha in 1812. Having captured the fortress, the son of Muhammad 'Ali Pasha destroyed it almost completely.

In 1995 the Supreme Council of Antiquities closed the building to the public and it can now only be admired from the deck of a boat.

231 top
A view of the courtyard in front of the underground section of the temple of Derr.

231 bottom
What remains of the fortress of Qasr Ibrim, built during the Roman Period.

Abu Simbel

Around 12 miles from Sudanese territory is one of the most well known of the Nubian sites, the great temple of Rameses II and the one dedicated to his beloved wife, Nefertari.

Towards the late 1960s, thanks to a remarkable engineering project, the temples were cut into blocks and rebuilt 213 feet higher up, set between two artificial hills and carefully positioned maintaining the original orientation, a condition indispensable to allow, as the pharaoh's architects intended, the sun's rays to penetrate the temple's inner chamber twice a year, bathing the four divinities, Ptah of Memphis, Amun-Ra of Thebes, Re-Horakty of Heliopolis, and the deified Rameses II himself, in its warm light.

The temple was "rediscovered" early in the nineteenth century by the Swiss explorer and traveler, J.L. Burckhardt, the first European since the Classical period to visit the site. To do so, he disguised himself as an Arab. A few years later, the Italian G.B. Belzoni managed to free the entrance to the temple from the sand, opening the way for many travelers to visit including celebrities such as the emperor Maximillian of Bavaria and Gustave Flaubert who, accompanied by the photographer Maxime du Camp, left us with valuable images of the temple facade, still partially

234-235
Rameses II dedicated the smaller temple at Abu Simbel to the goddess Hathor and his favorite wife, Nefertari.

234 bottom
Rameses II had himself represented no less than four times on the facade of his wife's temple.

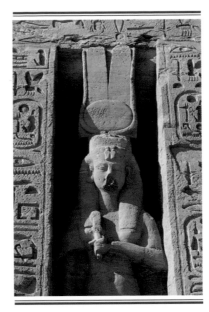

235 top

The two statues of Queen Nefertari portray her with the attributes of Hathor and the same size as her husband.

235 bottom

A general view of the two temples of Abu Simbel.

236-237

Both the Great and Small temples at Abu Simbel were moved to a hill approximately 230 yards from the west bank of the Nile, 210 feet higher than their original site.

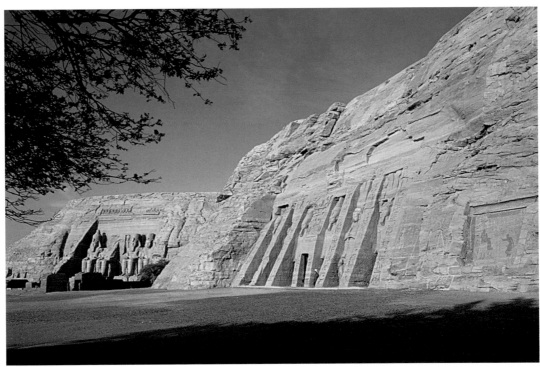

buried in the sand.

The temple was principally dedicated to Re-Horakty and originally featured four colossal statues of Rameses II observing the borders of Egypt with placid serenity. One of these collapsed, probably not long after its erection, due to an earthquake. Entering the first hall of the temple, one encounters a central nave flanked by Osirian pillars that recall the second courtyard of the Ramesseum. There follows a second, smaller hypostyle hall at the end of which are three chapels. The larger central one houses the four statues of the divinities.

The main theme in the temple decoration is the battle fought by Rameses II against the Hittites at Qadesh, an ancient town in Syria. Excavations and archaeological discoveries in the Hittite sites have greatly revised opinions regarding the king's victory, to the point where a rapid withdrawal of the Egyptian troops in the face of an efficient enemy ambush has even been hypothesized.

The smaller temple at Abu Simbel was dedicated to the goddess Hathor and Queen Nefertari, principal and beloved bride of the pharaoh. The facade of the small building features four statues of the king alternating with two of the queen in the guise of the goddess Hathor. Alongside them are the princes and princesses, sons and daughters of the great royal couple. Inside the temple, a single hypostyle hall is divided into three naves, each with six Hathoric pillars. There follows a small vestibule and a small shrine with Hathor in the form of a cow emerging from the rock wall to protect the pharaoh.

Serabit al-Khadem

Visiting the temple of Sarabit al-Khadem is not as simple and straightforward as a tourist fresh from visits to the temples of the fertile Nile valley might imagine. This site, built close to a number of turquoise, copper, and malachite mines, can in fact only be reached via a 20-mile asphalted road from the coast and a 7-mile drive aboard four-wheel drive vehicles along an unsurfaced track.

There is then an hour's trek to the top of the mountain from which the ancient temple overlooks the valley. Built during the Old Kingdom to offer spiritual protection to the workers in the various mines, and thus dedicated to the goddess Hathor in her manifestation as the "Lady of Turquoise," the Temple of Sarabit al-Khadem performed its task over the centuries and was embellished with a number of stelae and *ex-votos* during the Middle and New Kingdoms.

Among the relics from the Eighteenth Dynasty are the stelae of Thutmosis III and his co-ruler Queen Hatshepsut. Once Thutmosis was sole sovereign, he took Egyptian expansionism to its extreme, conquering and consolidating positions in foreign lands from which, as in this case, raw materials for religious, military, and civil purposes were extracted. Close to the main building, a second temple was later built and dedicated to Sopdu, a deity of the eastern desert.

In spite of the destruction caused by attempts to reopen a number of mines towards the middle of the nineteenth century, numerous fine stelae and bas-reliefs can still be seen at Sarabit al-Khadem. The turquoise that was mined here was taken along the valley of the

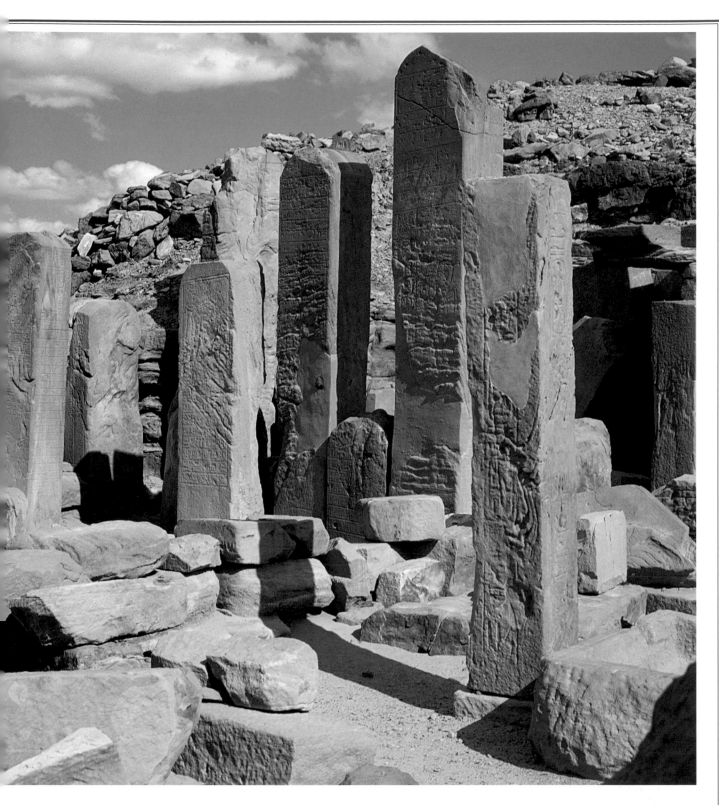

Wadi Mattala to the fortified port of
Al-Markha (a few miles to the south of Abu
Zenima) before being shipped to the green valley
of the Nile.

A mineral much sought-after by the ancient
Egyptians, it was used in the production of
necklaces and amulets and in powdered form as
a pigment.

246-247
A panoramic view of
the Monastery of
St. Catherine, enclosed
by powerful curtain walls.

246 *bottom left*
A view of the oasis that
extends in the vicinity of the
monastery, irrigated by a
perennial spring.

246 *bottom right*
The campanile of the church
of the Transfiguration rises
alongside the minaret of the
small mosque.

—— St. Catherine ——

247 top

The present-day monastery stands on the foundations of a fortress constructed in the first half of the sixth century by the emperor Justinian.

247 bottom

Two views from within the complex where around twenty monks currently live.

The Monastery of St. Catherine stands at an altitude of 5,151 feet in a valley at the foot of Gebel Musa, the Mountain of Moses, traditionally accepted as Mount Sinai. The fortress-monastery was built at the behest of Justinian between 527 and 547 A.D. to protect the hermits who had settled in this mountainous region of the Sinai from the attacks of the nomadic herders. Since then until the present day, the complex has enjoyed an unusual status. It was spared the consequences of invasions, even during the most intense period of Muslim domination of the area. Today, just as in the past,

the monks that administer the monastery—very hospitable but subject to severe regulations—are of Greek and Cypriot origins. Inside the irregular quadrilateral of the enclosure walls, partly dating back to the Byzantine era, are crowded buildings constructed during the long history of the monastery and they include a minaret which symbolizes the unusual tolerance that characterizes the institution. The buildings hugging the enclosure walls, partly used for the monks' and visitors' accommodation and administrative functions, also contain the library—rich in

manuscript codexes, but closed to the public—and the museum, which houses precious icons dating from the seventh to the eighteenth centuries. The functional structures gravitate around the church of the Transfiguration, a three-naved basilica that contains a precious Cretan iconostasis from the seventeenth century and the remains of St. Catherine. The parts of the complex associated with the oldest traditions are the biblical well "of Moses" or "of Jethro," and the Chapel of the Burning Bush where an ancient shrub marks the spot in which the prophet is said to have spoken with Yahweh. Near the monastery begins the path to Gebel Musa, a steep, partially stepped track that leads through the "Confession Gate" to the peak on which Moses is said to have received the Tablets of the Law, today occupied by two recent small buildings, a chapel and a mosque.

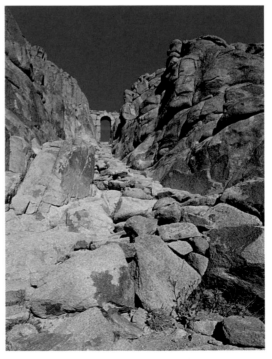

248
The central nave of the church of the Transfiguration, with the incredibly rich iconostasis.

249 top
One of the interiors of the monastic complex.

249 center and bottom left
On top of Gebel Musa is the chapel of the Holy Trinity.

249 bottom right
The summit of Mount Sinai can be reached passing below

the celebrated Confession Gate.

250-251
Saint Catherine's Monastery at the foot of Mount Sinai was founded where God revealed himself to Moses in the form of a burning bush.

Abaton: "inaccessible," indicates a subterranean area of a temple.

Amarna, Tell al-: modern name for the location of Akhenaten, "The Horizon of Aten," the new capital founded by Amenhotep IV - Akhenaten (1350-1333 B.C.).

Amduat: title of the most important funerary liturgical work of the New Kingdom, based on the sun's nocturnal journey through the Underworld, divided into twelve sections corresponding to the twelve night hours.

Amulet: generally small object intended to protect their owners during their terrestrial lives and in the next world, guaranteeing the conservation of the vital functions and certain qualities (health, wisdom, beauty, etc.).

Amun: member of the Theban Triad together with Mut and Khonsu. Also known as the "King of the Gods." Depicted in human form, occasionally ithyphallic (see *ithyphallic*) or as a ram, with two plumes on his head-dress.

Ankh: hieroglyphic symbol of life, a potent amulet.

Ansate: referring to vases and receptacles equipped with *ansae*, curved appendixes attached to the sides of vases or amphorae to act as handles or as decoration.

Anubis: jackal-headed deity presiding over mummification who escorted the deceased to the next world.

Apophis: serpent symbolizing the East, vainly attempts to swallow the sun every day at dawn.

Aten: the solar disc, depicted with multiple rays ending in hands, imposed by Akhenaten as the sole divinity.

Atum: deity representing the sun at dusk, identified as Ra-Atum, demiurge of Heliopolis.

Bastet: goddess represented in feline form, with a cat's head or rarely that of a lioness, presides over music and joy.

Bes: spirit of birth and infants, always depicted from the front and in a threatening pose to defeat evil demons.

Book of the Dead: illustrated collection of 190 chapters comprising the formulas that were said to guarantee the survival of the deceased in the underworld.

Burnisher: wooden tool, superficially carbonized, used to cover a metal surface with a protective oxide or sulphurous patina, the process being known as burnishing.

Cachette: "hiding place," refers in particular to the underground chambers in which royal mummies and parts of the funerary treasures were concealed to protect them from grave robbers.

Canopic vases: containers used for the internal organs of the mummified corpse. The funerary furnishings comprised four canopic vases, each of which was placed under the protection of one of the sons of Horus and frequently had a lid representing their features (man, baboon, dog, or falcon).

Cartouche: oval figure representing a length of cord containing the principal two of the sovereign's five names.

Criosphinx: sphinx (see *sphinx*) with a ram's head.

Crypt: hypogeum (see *hypogeum*) generally dedicated to sacred and funerary functions.

Demotic: "relating to the people, popular." Refers to the simplified form of hieroglyphic writing for general use.

Diorite: volcanic mineral of a dark color and exceptional hardness, used in architecture and statuary.

Dromos: the avenue giving access to the temples, frequently flanked by sphinxes (see *sphinx*).

Electrum: alloy of gold and silver.

Encaustic: a painting technique based on the use of pigments dissolved in melted wax and applied hot.

Faience: silica paste with a glassy appearance obtained by heating and mixing alkali, copper, and sodium; generally takes on a bluish color.

Geb: deity personifying the Earth, husband of Nut (see *Nut*).

Gebel: "mount," in Arabic.

Ged: pillar representing the backbone of Osiris and symbolizing stability and endurance.

Harakhty: see *Ra-Harakhty*.

Hathor: goddess frequently represented with the head of a cow and occasionally with just bovine ears, protected women, music, and the deceased.

Heb-sed: see *Sed*.

Heka-Kasutt: the "Princes of the Foreign Lands," name given by the Egyptians to the semi-nomadic Semite peoples (or perhaps to their leaders only) who penetrated Egypt in the 17th century B.C. and were expelled around a century later.

Hieratic: "relating to the sacred," within the ambit of ancient Egypt it refers in particular to the simplified transcription of hieroglyphic writing, a kind of cursive script used by priests and functionaries.

Hieroglyph: "sacred inscription," each symbol in the ancient Egyptian writing system, originally having an exclusively pictorial and ideographic value, later evolving into a phonetic form.

Horus: falcon-headed god, son of Osiris and Isis and nephew of Seth, the principal celestial deity protecting the sovereign and identified with him.

Horun: falcon-headed god, locally identified in the sphinx of Giza.

Hyksos: Greek transcription of Heka-Kasutt (see *Heka-Kasutt*).

Hypogeum: subterranean.

Hypostyle: vast hall with a flat roof supported by rows of columns.

Iconostasis: dividing screen typical of Greek Orthodox churches, separates the presbytery from the nave and is lavishly decorated with icons.

Intercolumniation: the space between two columns, either empty or occupied by a low wall.

Ithyphallic: "of the erect phallus," term relating to the phallic fertility cults.

Ka: one of the spirits of man, representing the life force. Created together with the individual, it survives the body after death, but depends on the same terrestrial conditions: the offerings of food, real or painted, left in the tombs are destined for the *Ka*.

Kush: Egyptian name for Nubia, a territory partly corresponding to present-day northern Sudan.

Mammisi: small temples characteristic of the Late Period erected alongside the principal temples and celebrating the birth of a god.

Mastaba: the oldest form of Egyptian surface tomb, built in stone or brick. The term means "bench" in Arabic, referring to the parallelepiped form of the building composed of one or more shrines from which the shaft or corridor leading to the underground burial chamber starts.

Migdol: fortification of Assyrian origin, the best preserved example of which is found at Western Thebes, in the funerary temple of Rameses III: a fortified gateway of a number of storeys, topped by Assyrian-style stepped battlements.

Min: ithyphallic (see *ithyphallic*) mummiform deity with the right arm raised and gripping a flail; protected the fertility and tracks of the Eastern Desert.

Montu: falcon-headed god of war.

Mut: bride of Amun, originally a vulture goddess, subsequently took on human form.

Naos: the internal part of the temple containing the statue of the divinity.

Neith: one of the goddesses of the funerary cult, together with Isis, Nephthys, and Selkis. Tutelary divinity, and since the New Kingdom also considered to have given birth to the sun.

Nemes: head-dress reserved for the sovereign, consisting of a striped fabric cap with two flaps either side of the face.

Nephthys: sister of Isis and consort of Seth, the god who killed Osisris.

Nilometer: building containing a graduated pillar destined to measure the level reached by the Nile during the seasonal flood. Its main function was that of calculating in advance the taxable entity of the forthcoming harvest.

Nomarch: high ranking functionary governing a nome (see *nome*).

Nome: administrative area of

ancient Egypt; according to the period, the nomes numbered between 38 and 42.

Nun: chaos, the primordial ocean from the waters of which rose the Sky and the Earth.

Nut: personification of the celestial vault, bride of Geb (see *Geb*). Depicted with an arching body and decorated with a cluster of stars.

Opening of the mouth: ceremony designed to restore life to the effigy through the touch of a small instrument representing an axe.

Opet: a religious festival held during the third month of the flood: the celebrations focused on the transportation by boat of the statue of Amun from the Temple of Karnak to the Temple of Luxor dedicated to him and known as "Ipet-resit," or Southern Harem (of Amun).

Osiris: mummiform god who presided over the Underworld; husband and brother of Isis, killed by his brother Seth and after his death magically conceived Horus (see *Horus*), the falcon-god who avenged him.

Ostracon: clay fragment used as a support for brief notes and inscriptions.

Pronaos: vestibule of a temple or tomb.

Ptah: creator god of Memphis. Depicted as mummiform and bearing a sceptre. Consort of Sekhmet, the lioness goddess, and over the course of time was syncretized with the Memphis funerary deity, Sokaris.

Punt: Egyptian name for a territory situated in East Africa (variously identified as Somalia, Eritrea, or southern Sudan) towards which were despatched commercial

expeditions from the 5th Dynasty (2465-2323 B.C.) onwards. The best known expedition was that ordered by Queen Hatshepsut (1479-1458 B.C., 18th Dynasty), depicted in a magnificent bas-relief from Deir al-Bahari.

Pylon: monumental entrance to the Egyptian temples, composed of two trapezoidal towers on either side of a gateway.

Pyramid texts: formulas relating to the sovereign's funerary ritual, present in the pyramids from the late 5th Dynasty through to the end of the 6th.

Pyramidion: a solar symbol, a miniature pyramid in stone, frequently gilded or covered with electrum (see *electrum*) and located at the tip of an obelisk or in place of the apex of a pyramid.

Qasr: "castle" in Arabic. From the plural noun, *uqsor*, derives the name of Luxor, a corruption of al-Uqsor, "The Castles."

Ra: extremely ancient sun deity of Heliopolis. During the day Ra had the head of a falcon overlooked by the solar disc while during his nocturnal journey (see *Amduat*) he had a ram's head.

Ra-Horakhty: syncretic divine figure with the appearance of a falcon and equipped with a solar disc. Unites Ra and Horus in a deity of the two horizons (east and west).

Rostaw: indicates in the funerary texts the "paths of the Underworld" followed by the deceased between the fourth and the fifth hours of the night, a sector dominated by Sokar, god of the necropolis of Memphis; in geographical terms, identified the Giza plateau.

Sacellum: place of worship in a segregated or hidden room.

Sanctuary: the innermost area of the temple, the tabernacle.

Sarcophagus texts: collection of formulas intended to guarantee the survival of the deceased in the Underworld, inscribed on the sarcophagi from the First Intermediate Period through to the Middle Kingdom.

Schist: metamorphic rock composed of parallel strata.

Sed: the jubilee festival celebrated by sovereigns in the thirtieth year of their reign and subsequently at shorter intervals of between five and three years.

Sekhmet: lioness goddess, protector of the royal power of the sovereign; occasionally assimilated with Bastet, Hathor, and Isis, but possesses a darker connotation than the other goddesses.

Serapis: Ptolemaic deity combining the characteristics of Osiris and Olympian attributes, particularly those of the figure of Zeus.

Seth: god of chaotic forces, brother and killer of Osiris (see *Osiris*), particularly venerated in the delta. Depicted in human form and with the head of an unrecognizable animal, perhaps an anteater or a greyhound.

Shawabty: statuette, frequently made of blue faience (see *faience*), destined to replace the owner in the agriculture labors of the Underworld.

Sistrum: musical instrument similar to a rattle, sacred to Hathor and Bastet.

Sobek: crocodile god, depicted both in human form with the head of the reptile, and in completely animal form.

Sphinx: embodiment of royal power with a lion's body and human male head. Located to

guard the doors of temples and along the *dromos* (see *dromos*).

Steatite: compact variety of mineral talcum also known as soapstone. Greenish in color and easily worked.

Stela: stone or wood slab carrying inscriptions and designs linked with the various functions performed: celebratory, funerary, propagandistic, and boundary marking.

Sycamore: tree sacred to Hathor (see *Hathor*) and Nut (see *Nut*); very hard wood used to make furniture, sarcophagi, and other funerary accessories.

Ta-set-Neferu: ancient Egyptian name for the present day Valley of the Queens variously interpreted as meaning "Place of Beauty," "of Splendors," or "of Lotuses."

Teken: Egyptian name for the obelisks.

Tell: Arabic term indicating an artificial mound created by the superimposition of the ruins of a settlement.

Thot: deity depicted in human form with the head of an ibex or in the form of the bird, or again in the form of a baboon. Protector of scribes and the sciences, considered to be the inventor of writing.

Udjat: the eye of Horus, a protective amulet.

Uraeus: the cobra, symbol of royalty.

Wadi: the dry bed of a stream typical of the desert areas of North Africa and the Middle East, flooded only during the seasonal rains. In Arabic, it is close to the term meaning "valley."

Wadjet: tutelary goddess of Lower Egypt, takes the form of a *uraeus*.

Index

Illustration credits